On Professions,
Professionals,
and
Professional
Ethics

On
Professions,
Professionals,
and
Professional Ethics

RONALD C. HORN, Ph.D., CPCU, CLU
Ben H. Williams Professor of Insurance Studies
Hankamer School of Business, Baylor University

First Edition • 1978

AMERICAN INSTITUTE FOR
PROPERTY AND LIABILITY UNDERWRITERS
720 Providence Road, Malvern, Pennsylvania 19355-0770

© 1978

AMERICAN INSTITUTE FOR
PROPERTY AND LIABILITY UNDERWRITERS, INC.

Third Printing ● January 1989

Library of Congress Catalog Number 78-67501
International Standard Book Number 0-89463-020-2

Printed in the United States of America

To my father,
Claude J. Horn,
A giant among those whom history
will record as larger men,
And to all parents like him,
For their impeccable integrity.

Foreword

The American Institute for Property and Liability Underwriters and the Insurance Institute of America are companion, nonprofit, educational organizations supported by the property-liability insurance industry. Their purpose is to provide quality continuing education programs for insurance personnel.

The American Institute maintains and administers the program leading to the Chartered Property Casualty Underwriter (CPCU)® professional designation.

The Insurance Institute of America offers a wide range of associate designation and certificate programs in the following technical and managerial disciplines:

> Accredited Adviser in Insurance (AAI)®
> Associate in Claims (AIC)
> Associate in Underwriting (AU)
> Associate in Risk Management (ARM)
> Associate in Loss Control Management (ALCM)®
> Associate in Premium Auditing (APA)®
> Associate in Management (AIM)
> Associate in Research and Planning (ARP)®
> Associate in Insurance Accounting and Finance (AIAF)
> Associate in Automation Management (AAM)
> Associate in Marine Insurance Management (AMIM)
> Certificate in General Insurance
> Certificate in Supervisory Management
> Certificate in Introduction to Claims
> Certificate in Introduction of Property and Liability Insurance

Throughout the history of the CPCU program, an annual updating of parts of the course of study took place. But as changes in the insurance industry came about at an increasingly rapid pace, and as the world in which insurance operates grew increasingly complex, it became clear that a thorough, fundamental revision of the CPCU curriculum was necessary.

The American Institute began this curriculum revision project by organizing a committee of academicians, industry practitioners, and

Institute staff members. This committee was charged with the responsibility of determining and stating those broad goals which should be the educational aims of the CPCU program in contemporary society. With these goals formulated, the curriculum committee began writing specific educational objectives which were designed to achieve the stated goals of the program. This was a time-consuming and difficult task. But this process made certain that the revised CPCU curriculum would be based on a sound and relevant foundation.

Once objectives were at least tentatively set, it was possible to outline a new, totally revised and reorganized curriculum. These outlines were widely circulated and the reactions of more than 1,800 educators and industry leaders were solicited, weighed, and analyzed. These outlines were then revised and ultimately became the structure of the new, ten-course curriculum.

With the curriculum design in hand, it was necessary to search for study materials which would track with the revised program's objectives and follow its design. At this stage of curriculum development, the Institute reached the conclusion that it would be necessary for the Institute to prepare and publish study materials specifically tailored to the revised program. This conclusion was not reached hastily. After all, for the Institute to publish textbooks and study materials represents a significant broadening of its traditional role as an examining organization. But the unique educational needs of CPCU candidates, combined with the lack of current, suitable material available through commercial publishers for use in some areas of study, made it necessary for the Institute to broaden its scope to include publishing.

Throughout the development of the CPCU text series, it has been—and will continue to be—necessary to draw on the knowledge and skills of Institute staff members. These individuals will receive no royalties on texts sold, and their writing responsibilities are seen as an integral part of their professional duties. We have proceeded in this way to avoid any possibility of conflicts of interests. This particular ethics essay was authored entirely by Dr. Ronald C. Horn, CPCU, CLU, a well-known insurance educator. He will receive no royalties on the publication, but he received nominal compensation for writing the essay.

All Institute textbooks have been—and will continue to be—subjected to an extensive review process. Reviewers are drawn from both industry and academic ranks. All published ethics materials are also approved by the Board of Ethical Inquiry, as is required by the Institute Bylaws.

We invite and will welcome any and all criticisms of our publications. It is only with such comments that we can hope to provide high quality educational texts, materials, and programs.

Norman A. Baglini, Ph.D., CPCU, CLU, AU
President

Preface

The American Institute commissioned me to write this volume and direct it to the educational objectives which had been approved for the professional ethics segment of the revised CPCU curriculum. On the subjects of professions, professionalism, professional ethics, and written codes of ethics, there are literally hundreds of publications well worth reading. For those so inclined, extensive citations are provided in the footnotes and the bibliography. CPCU candidates will not be examined on readings which are not assigned. However, I especially recommend, as optional supplementary reading, the new book referred to often in this essay, *The Ethical Basis of Economic Freedom,* an anthology of excellent articles edited by Ivan Hill.

In Chapter 4, I have named many of the Institute staff members, Trustees and committee members who contributed to the development and adoption of the American Institute's Code of Professional Ethics. A special role was played by the very special Melvin A. Holmes, CPCU, Harold Eckmann, and Porter Ellis, CPCU, members of the Ethics Policy Committee of the Board. They are the epitome of professionalism in its finest sense, and the respect and confidence they enjoy from fellow Trustees are what ultimately enabled the new Code to become a reality. I would also like to express my personal gratitude to the current members of the Institute's Board of Ethical Inquiry: H. Paul Carpenter, CPCU, CLU, Caleb L. Fowler, CPCU, John H. Ellen, CPCU, Clifford J. Jefferies, CPCU, John Langeland, CPCU, Rie R. Sharp, CPCU, John P. Young, CPCU, CLU, and the Ethics Counsel, Dr. Frederick R. Hodosh, CPCU, who serves as nonvoting Chairman, Ex Officio. The members of the Board of Ethical Inquiry provided me with much-needed encouragement and sound advice. They also approved the general content of this volume, as is required by the Institute Bylaws. Even so, except where otherwise specifically noted, the opinions expressed herein are my own personal opinions. They do *not* necessarily represent the opinions of the Institute, the Society of CPCU, the Board of Ethical Inquiry, its individual members, other committees or boards of the Institute, committees or boards of the Society or its chapters, or any other CPCU.

Because most of the important *concepts* contained in this volume are inherently dialectical, as explained more fully in the text, the work is in the nature of a formal essay. I have raised many questions and posed many issues. Though I have supplied very few answers, I have made no attempt to conceal my own judgments. I have tried not to misrepresent or oversimplify the positions taken by other writers. I have made a case for my own strongly-held views on professionalism. Therein lies the dilemma of a teacher in his role as an advocate or salesman. Because he seeks to persuade, he is inclined to work hardest on the merits of his own case, leaving it largely up to others to file counter-briefs. Or, in trying so hard to be "objective," he leaves the impression that all positions are equally meritorious. The latter can be even more misleading than the former, particularly as respects dialectical concepts which can be defined only by the rhetoric of taking sides. It is no defense for me to admit that I am probably guilty on both counts. But there is some comfort in the realization that perceptive readers will see through any inadvertent sham with sharp and terrible eyes.

In keeping with a nice tradition, I give warm thanks to my wife, Karen, for typing the manuscript several times, and to Kristine, Andrew, and Kimberly, our three children, for patiently enduring a lengthy period of inconvenience and frustration. It all seemed worthwhile to the older members of our family, if only because it inspired the nine-year-old daughter to write a "book" with her crayons. My sincere thanks also go to all members of the American Institute family, for enduring me as a consultant over a period of nearly fifteen years.

Ronald C. Horn
Richmond, Kentucky
February 27, 1978

Table of Contents

CHAPTER 1

The Idea of a Profession

Thus it happens that rhetoric is an offshoot of dialectic and also of ethical studies.
—Aristotle, *Rhetoric.*

With due regard to the etymological origins of words, the dictionaries dutifully record that the term profession is a derivative of the Latin "professio," which means an open or public declaration, avowal, acknowledgment, or affirmation. The term was first applied narrowly to the vow of consecration made by a person entering a religious order, and it was later broadened to include virtually any kind of solemn declaration. These literal senses of profession, which are still very much a part of our language, continue to be included among the various dictionary definitions. Moreover, their intended meaning is normally quite clear in the specific context of a user, as when a clergyman speaks of a "profession of faith" or a person (using the verb form) "professes" to be an expert in a particular field. No serious definitional problems are posed by such uses. They are still widely accepted on their merits as a proper means of conveying the notion of an open or public declaration.

It is otherwise with the vocational senses of profession. In fact, the vocational senses of profession have provoked widespread disagreement and controversy. Although the word profession was used to mean a "learned vocation" as early as 1541, its meaning had already been generalized, some thirty-five years later, to indicate "any calling or occupation by which a person habitually earns his living."[1] Both uses

---

1. Morris L. Cogan, "Toward a Definition of Profession," *Harvard Educational Review,* Vol. XXIII, No. 1 (Winter, 1953), p. 34. It is little wonder that this well-documented article is frequently cited by contemporary writers. With an analysis that draws on a variety of disciplines, the author has done an admirable job of bringing the concept of profession into focus.

1

have been preserved in our modern language and compounded by additional variations. For instance, it takes only a casual sampling of dictionaries to reveal that people now use the word profession to mean (1) "a vocation or occupation requiring advanced training in some liberal art or science, and usually involving mental rather than manual work, as teaching, engineering, writing, etc.; especially, medicine, law, or theology" (formerly called *the learned professions*), (2) "a principal calling, vocation, or employment," and/or (3) "the collective body of persons engaged in or practicing a particular calling or vocation."[2] The third of these meanings is not really disputed. Rather, the source of the current controversy is reflected in the inherent conflict between the first and second meanings. Critics contend that the word profession should not be applied to just any vocation. It should be reserved exclusively for particular vocations with clearly specified characteristics. Thus, for those who are not satisfied with contradictory generalizations, the dictionaries offer little more than a convenient point of departure.

The search for further clarification of the occupational concept of profession has prompted a number of writers to review the legal definitions which are provided in law dictionaries and court decisions. While such a review can be a valuable undertaking for some purposes, it is apparent that nonlegal scholars are more impressed by the shortcomings of legal definitions than they are by their virtues. As Professor Cogan succinctly put it, "The legal definitions are so closely shackled to the unique conditions of litigation that they are not generally applicable."[3]

Cogan's conclusion should be generalized, however, because there is always a close link between definitions and their purposes, whether or not it is made explicit. It is a link which renders many definitions useless beyond their intended purpose(s). The latter point is well illustrated by the various occupational definitions and classifications of the United States Departments of Labor and Commerce.[4] However useful

---

2. The first and third meanings were extracted from *Webster's New Twentieth Century Dictionary,* unabridged 2nd ed., 1975 (William Collins + World Publishing Co., Inc.), whereas the second meaning was taken from *Webster's Seventh New Collegiate Dictionary,* 1973 (G & C Merriam Co.). Other dictionaries contain meanings with somewhat different emphasis or phrasing, but the differences did not seem large enough to justify the space which would have been required to list them here.

3. Morris L. Cogan, op. cit., at p. 47.

4. See the *Dictionary of Occupational Titles,* 4th ed., 1977, U.S. Department of Labor, Employment and Training Administration; and, the rather different approach in "Occupations of Persons with High Earnings," 1970 Census of Population, U.S. Department of Commerce, Social and Economic Statistics Administration.

they may be for the purposes of government, the classifications tend to obscure the idea of a profession with an arbitrary and internally inconsistent system that raises more questions than it answers. Members of some occupations must surely wonder why they are excluded, without adequate explanation, from the professional category. And members of well-established professions like law and medicine will find themselves lumped together with some strange bedfellows.[5]

These introductory comments are merely (1) to identify our primary concern, the *idea* or concept of a profession, in its occupational sense, and (2) to suggest that it is not an easy concept to circumscribe with precise boundaries. It is no criticism to acknowledge that this idea does not readily emerge from dictionaries, legal definitions, or government classification systems. Indeed, the struggle to define the profession concept has led some writers to conclude that a precise statement is not possible. A larger number point to the lack of agreement on any one statement, and virtually all are forced to acknowledge the problems involved in formulating an acceptable definition.[6]

THE NATURE AND SIGNIFICANCE OF THE DEFINITIONAL PROBLEMS

One can easily appreciate why some writers have refused to venture a definition of profession. But those who assert that the concept is impossible to define have overstated the case. Though it undoubtedly would be very difficult to arrive at total agreement on any one definition (of nearly any concept), there is now substantial agreement, among serious students of the subject, on the key elements of the profession concept.

For instance, there is almost total agreement on the need to reject,

---

5. For example, the Commerce Department publication, *supra,* has a category called "professional, technical and kindred workers," which lumps physicians, lawyers and teachers with designers, musicians, painters, photographers and entertainers. Insurance agents, brokers and underwriters are classified as "sales workers," whereas insurance adjusters are put into the category of "clerical and kindred workers." Insurance managers and administrators will find themselves in the same occupational classification as wholesale and retail buyers, cafeteria and bar managers, funeral directors and building superintendents.

6. For a penetrating analysis, see Morris L. Cogan, "The Problem of Defining a Profession," *The Annals of the American Academy of Political and Social Science,* January 1955, pp. 105 et seq. In this article, Cogan builds upon his earlier work (see footnote No. 1) and provides a number of additional insights.

categorically, the notion that a profession is *any* principal calling, vocation, or employment. To do otherwise would relegate the idea of a profession to a mere synonym for words that need no help, and it would leave no other existing word that would be as adequate in referring to the *particular kind* of occupation most writers have in mind. Perhaps this is why the majority of writers do not feel the point is worth mentioning. They implicitly concentrate on defining a particular kind of occupation. Second, there is likewise almost universal agreement on the proposition that no single characteristic will adequately convey the idea of a profession. It follows that there is agreement on the general structure of a definition; namely, that a profession is an occupation which has specified characteristics. There is some disagreement as to exactly what these characteristics should be, and perhaps even more disagreement on the *degree* to which an occupation should possess the specified characteristics; nonetheless, the areas of agreement substantially diminish the definitional problems that would otherwise exist.

Before reviewing the various characteristics which have been suggested, it would first seem advisable to examine the question of why the remaining aspects of a definition are so controversial. Why, indeed, is it so difficult to reach agreement? Few writers have provided satisfactory answers to such questions (which may be one of the subtle reasons why differences of opinion persist).

In this writer's view, much of the disagreement flows from the fundamental and seldom-acknowledged truth that the term "profession" is what Richard Weaver undoubtedly would have called a "dialectical" term.[7] Dialectical terms stand for concepts; they are defined and made meaningful by their negatives or privations. Terms like "justice," "poor," and "unethical" are illustrative. They are positional terms reflecting the user's judgments of value. A person who employs such a term is at once engaged in an argument.

Weaver stressed the importance of distinguishing between dialectical terms and positive terms. "Positive" terms merely designate things which exist in the objective world, e.g., the tree, the table, the desk. Arguments over positive terms are not really arguments in the true sense, because they can be settled quickly by using an agreed-upon measure, just as one might settle a disagreement over the width of a desk by using a mutually acceptable yardstick. Such is not the case with dialectical terms. They belong to the world of ideas. For example, to say

---

7. Richard Weaver, *The Ethics of Rhetoric,* 1st Gateway ed. (Chicago: Henry Regnery Co., 1967), pp. 187-88. Weaver was but one of many philosophers, including Aristotle, who wrote about the nature of dialectical terms. Such philosophers were generally referring to "rhetoric" as the art of persuasion in pursuit of truth, the process of which necessarily involves dialectical terms.

that a family has an annual income of $10,000 is positive; to say that the same family is "underprivileged" is dialectical. It can be under-privileged only in reference to families that have more privileges.

Thus, if we are to understand the problem of defining profession, the difficulties in reaching an agreement on its meaning and the underlying nature of the concept, we should first acknowledge that profession is a dialectical term. It is a positional term which reflects the user's judg-ments of value. To say that profession is one thing is to join in argument with all those who contend that it is something else. This is because the term profession stands for a concept which owes its very existence, not to the external world, but to the world of ideas. The process of defining profession is inherently a dialectical process. As such, it is defined by taking sides, by taking a position on what it is and what it is not. If ten persons are to agree on a particular definition of the profession concept, they must be convinced of its merits.

Some writers do not even try to offer a convincing case. They dismiss the matter rather casually, either on the evasive grounds that "there is no best definition" or by the shallow contention that the controversy is "purely a matter of semantics." Such writers seem especially inclined to use the expedient of declaring (that) "for the purposes of this discussion, profession will be defined as . . . .," thus implying that the only impor-tant thing is to be consistent in one's own context. The declarative approach has a communications value, but it is no substitute for a convincing argument of the merits.

Among those who do try to persuade others to accept a particular definition, some probably fail because they overlook one important aspect of a dialectical position; namely, that it is based, necessarily, on presuppositions or assumptions. Hence, what is apparently a disagree-ment about a definition is often just a disagreement about the funda-mental assumption(s) upon which it is based. An example can be found in the tendency to assert that "the following characteristics of a profes-sion are generally agreed upon." Forget the fact that we are not told exactly who has agreed. Instead, let us suppose that the statement is true, at least in the sense that 51 out of 100 knowledgeable adults agree. If the writer goes on to suggest that these *are* therefore the characteris-tics, he is presupposing or *assuming* that the concept is defined by a simple majority vote, an assumption with which some will not agree.

Even when assumptions are made explicit and supported by a logical rationale, there is no assurance that either the definitions or the as-sumptions will be accepted. Profession is not only a dialectic term. It also provokes strong emotions in some quarters. As Morris Cogan has ob-served: "To define 'profession' is to invite controversy. . . . When defini-tions of it are proposed they are rarely subjected to rational consideration. Reactions tend to be polarized toward an enthusiastic and uncritical acceptance or toward a rancorous and defensive rejection. So many advantages have accrued to profession, so many claims to it are made by so many people, that the cutting edge of a definition—be it ever so blunt—is almost sure to draw cries of protest from many aspirants to the title."[8] Among other things, Cogan's remarks focus our attention on what might be called a verbal "tug of war between the haves and the have nots." Whereas the professions have (or are perceived to have) rank, privileges, and high social status in western civilization, various other occupations do not. At least some professionals, apparently bent on preserving the status quo, show a tendency to oppose the broadening of the profession concept in a way that would include other individuals and groups. One finds a hint of this attitude in the support for raising admission standards, as well as in the use of such terms as "true"professions and "pseudo" professions. On the other hand, among those engaged in occupations which have not been widely accepted as professions, there is a strong drive to appear professional, if only because of their aspirations for status. The professional is believed to wear a badge of prestige, in effect, and this has inspired many individuals and groups to seek the distinction.

The long-standing social status of the professions was confirmed in a recent Harris poll, which asked 1,520 American adults how they view the prestige of various occupations.[9] Of interest here are the indications of the proportion of adults who feel that a given occupation either has "very great prestige" or "considerable prestige." Scientists headed the list of the fifteen occupations rated. Some 91 percent of the persons surveyed perceived scientists as having "very great or considerable prestige." Comparable percentages for other groups were doctors (90 percent), ministers (73 percent), lawyers (73 percent), teachers (65 percent), and athletes (58 percent). At the bottom of the list were politicians (42 percent) and salesmen [sic] (25 percent). Harris observed that public confidence in lawyers had declined, compared to earlier surveys, and that the prestige of athletes has grown along with their compensation.

Why are these occupations perceived to have prestige and social status? Although a satisfactory explanation is well beyond the scope of this paper, a few observations may serve the less ambitious task of provoking some thought and reflection. One thing worth thinking about is the extent to which the public's view of prestige and social status is influenced by monetary considerations. In a society which is achieve-

---

8. Morris L. Cogan, "The Problem of Defining a Profession," op. cit., p. 105.
9. From an article by Louis Harris, *Chicago Tribune* release, January 12, 1978.

ment oriented, and in which so many persons regard income and wealth as a measure of success, there is doubtless some connection between financial success and prestige. This may partially explain the prestige of such groups as physicians and "professional" athletes, but it fails to account for the relatively high prestige of teachers and ministers (most of whom are not very high on the income scale) and the relatively low prestige of some types of salespersons (some of whom are at the very top of the income scale). Cogan probably brings us closer to the heart of the matter when he observes (in theology, law, and medicine) that "the traditional professions mediate man's relations to God, man's relations to man and state, and man's relations to his biological environment. . . . The practitioner's activities, then, impinge radically upon the most basic concerns of man. Such a concept might help explain the value, status, privilege, and power that have accrued to profession. These are considerations that would tend to become attached to the experts who serve the vital needs of mankind."[10] A slight modification of Cogan's hypothesis would be that the public tends to accept as a profession (and view as prestigious) occupations which the *public perceives to be essential* in serving the basic concerns of mankind. To this we ought to add that the public generally seems to look with greater admiration upon occupations which require extensive preparation and training, though not necessarily in direct proportion thereto. If these partial and tentative explanations have any validity, it would seem that some aspirants to professional status may find it to be beyond their immediate reach. At least they will not be able to achieve it merely with self-serving titles and definitions. Instead, their ultimate burden may be to *prove* (a) that they serve the basic concerns of mankind, and (b) that they are equipped to do so by meaningful preparation and training.

Returning to the central point, it has been suggested that the problem of defining profession is a problem of resolving the remaining disagreements on its outside boundaries. The resolution of such disagreements is by nature a dialectical process, since profession is a dialectical term. It also provokes rather strong emotions among both aspirants and traditional possessors of the profession status. However, as we shall see in the next section, there is considerable agreement on the desirable attributes or traits of a profession. The emotional barriers to agreement seem strongest when it comes to the matter of deciding whether a particular occupation *adequately meets* these traits or characteristics. Part of the difficulty is in deciding on *what* the test of adequacy should be. Yet, even if that can be resolved, there is still the practical problem of *measuring* the degree to which various characteristics are present. There is a sense in which these latter two difficulties are not

---

10. Morris L. Cogan, "Toward a Definition of Profession," op. cit., p. 36.

problems of definition per se. But there is another sense in which they are, if only because the traits in question are not absolutes. They are relatives, i.e., they come in degrees. One either possesses an automobile or one does not; one possesses competence, honesty, and other such traits only in degrees. The question of relativity or degree gets even more involved, of course, when a *group* of persons is measured against a group of traits.

In this writer's opinion, the foregoing analysis leads to two tentative but inescapable conclusions. First, we may never be able to resolve, with any finality, whether this occupation or that *is* a "profession," or even whether it *deserves* to be thought of as a profession. Public opinion polls may reflect the perceptions of the majority at any specific time, but the underlying idea of a profession is not defined by passing the ballot box. Second and more important, the idea of a profession has already been sufficiently well defined to serve as a set of ideals, a set of ideals which *all* individuals can aspire to achieve in their daily occupational pursuits. This may ultimately be the primary value of defining profession. If so, it is a value which alone justifies further attempts to clarify the idea and reduce it to more functional specifics.

CHARACTERISTICS OF A PROFESSION

In their efforts to delineate the idea of a profession, a great many writers have concentrated on identifying the distinguishing characteristics. What characteristics, traits, or attributes, they ask, distinguish a profession from other occupations? Their answers commonly take the form of a list of characteristics which professions are thought to possess.[11] While some writers explicitly or implicitly treat the characteristics as literal "prerequisites," this is probably just a poor choice of words, since most see the need to accommodate the varying degrees in which the characteristics may realistically be found in any one occupational group. The majority of writers also seem to feel that it is the collective of all characteristics, taken together, that combine to form the ultimate test. That is to say, it is seldom claimed that any one characteristic is *unique* to the professions, but rather that the combined set of

11. Of the numerous publications which could be cited here, one of the most engaging and praiseworthy of the contemporary efforts is that of Edwin S. Overman, *The Professional Concept and Business Ethics,* the American Institute for Property and Liability Underwriters, Inc. The late Dr. S.S. Huebner, along with the late Dr. Harry J. Loman, left countless admirers and legacies, but their contributions to the professionalization of the insurance industry were perhaps their most priceless gifts to future generations.

characteristics is unique enough to distinguish professions from other occupations. Where do the lists of characteristics originate? There are a few creative products of careful thought and reflection. There are also some self-serving lists which were apparently contrived to persuade others that their authors' occupations are professions. However, the majority have been content to use medicine, law, and theology—the so-called "learned professions"—as models or benchmarks. The usual line of reasoning goes something like this: the learned professions were the first "true" professions to be widely recognized as such; they have continued to be thought of as professions over a long period of time; they have identifiable characteristics; and, therefore, these characteristics can be taken as the characteristics of a true profession. What is left unspoken is the fact that the characteristics usually identified are not all of the characteristics of the learned professions. They are mainly what are thought to be the *desirable* characteristics of law, medicine, and theology. This does not mean they are accepted uncritically by everyone (e.g., many have questioned certain aspects of the lawyer-client and physician-patient relationships). What it does mean is that there has been no conscious effort to use *un*desirable characteristics as a model for others to follow.

A complete inventory of the characteristics which have been suggested would occupy the better part of a thick book. It might also prove tedious to readers, and it probably would be an unnecessary distraction from the notions which are primary to the idea of a profession. Hence, what follows is a brief sample of views on the desirable characteristics of a profession.

A Commitment to High Ethical Standards

We will have much more to say about ethics in later sections of this monograph. Here, suffice it to say that on one point there is virtually no disagreement. A sincere commitment to high ethical standards is an essential characteristic of every true profession. Indeed, this characteristic is a literal prerequisite. Without it, a profession would be little more than a way to earn a living. Surely a profession must be more than that, if it is to have any meaning and purpose at all.

A Prevailing Attitude of Altruism

A profession is also said to be characterized by a prevailing attitude of altruism. "Altruism" is a term first used, we are told, by the

Positivists who were followers of the French philosopher, Comte. It means *unselfish concern for the welfare of others,* and it is the polar opposite of "egoism," the doctrine that self-interest is the proper goal of all human actions. While there is a significant degree of overlap between altruism and a commitment to high ethical standards, altruism is often treated as being especially worthy of separate mention. It also shares with ethical standards the property of being more easily "professed" than achieved. Yet, the case for altruism rests on its inherent virtues as a desirable standard of human conduct, on its intrinsic worth as a goal, apart from the obstacles to its ultimate achievement. It is at once a case for the basic goodness of "charity," in its ancient sense of love, and a goal shared by nearly every major religion throughout the history of civilization.

What remains is the question of whether a profession is distinguished by an unselfish concern for the welfare of others. Since no profession can make good the claim that *all* of its members are constantly motivated by a spirit of altruism, it seems clear that the proponents of this characteristic are either naive or they are referring to an abstract ideal which has no counterpart in reality, other than where it can be identified as a prevailing attitude among members of an occupational group. It also seems clear that most proponents are using the term altruism, somewhat loosely, to convey the antithesis of "mercenary." A truly mercenary occupation is one which is pursued solely for money or other personal gain. A profession is not a mercenary occupation, it is argued, because it is pursued largely out of an unselfish desire to serve the needs of others, apart from any hope or expectation of financial or personal gain.

Although serving the vital needs of mankind may well be the most important societal value of professions, it does not necessarily follow that professions can claim exclusive rights to the role. Nor does it follow that professions are pursued largely for unselfish reasons. Skeptics still have ample reason to suspect that comparatively few persons would pursue law or medicine if doing so offered no opportunity for social status or large financial rewards (or to wonder whether more persons might aspire to the clergy if it virtually guaranteed them a spot at the top of the income distribution). Accordingly, it is probably more accurate to say that professions offer the *opportunity* to make a living by doing worthwhile things for which there are many rewards, including the rewards which are intrinsic to the nature of the work. Even this formulation does not, by itself, distinguish professions from other occupations. Nearly all occupational pursuits offer at least some personal rewards, other than money, and they may include rewards which are as satisfying as those enjoyed by professions. Against this it is argued that the pursuits of professions are somehow more worthwhile than other rewarding occupational pursuits, in that professions are necessarily involved in providing services to meet the vital needs of mankind. True, when a surgeon saves a young girl's life, an attorney protects her legal rights, or a clergyman gives her moral guidance and comfort, they are obviously meeting vital needs, and they are more to be admired than one who gets satisfaction from murdering for hire. But to assert that professions are therefore unique occupations can reach the stage of an arrogant and condescending attitude which contradicts the very claim to altruism. Is the lawyer who handles the legalities of a divorce serving a more vital human need than the bricklayer who builds a church, the artist who creates the timeless masterpiece, the business executive whose genius and drive create employment for thousands, the scientist who discovers a new source of energy, or the farmer whose crops feed the hungry? Which of these pursuits are the most worthy? The least worthy? Can the worthiness of pursuits serve as a meaningful basis for distinguishing professions from other occupations? In any occupational group, can it be determined whether an attitude of altruism prevails over purely mercenary goals? Such questions are not easily answered. But they do pose issues which suggest an uneasy alliance between traditional professions and the attribute of altruism.

At best, a prevailing attitude of altruism, the striving to be guided by larger values than purely mercenary ends, is a goal which traditional professions cannot claim uniquely for themselves. The idea of a profession may be partially characterized by the intrinsic nature of the work, as well as by its ultimate goal. But the same can be said of other worthwhile pursuits. Thus, the notion of profession does not fully emerge until we consider its additional characteristics.

Mandatory Educational Preparation and Training

Beginning with the earliest use of the phrase "learned" profession and continuing to the present day, a notion which has reigned largely unchallenged is that professions are distinguished by the extensive education and training required of their members. This characteristic is normally treated as a mandatory or required precondition of profession membership, and it is often said or taken to mean the specific preconditions of collegiate-level degrees, apprenticeship requirements, and qualifying examinations. For example, individuals can practice medicine only if they *first* graduate from medical school, satisfy internship and residency requirements, and pass the various examinations which set the qualifying standards. The use of the term "practice" is noteworthy in this context, because the preponderance of opinion would reserve the profession classification for occupations which involve practical application of skills.[12] However, proponents of the latter view are quick to point out that the skill ingredient produces only a partial overlap between professions and the crafts. The work of crafts is primarily manual in nature, whereas the work of professions is primarily mental in nature. More important, the skills applied by professions are said to be based upon theoretical knowledge, analysis and understanding.

Alfred North Whitehead regarded theory as the very essence of the idea of a profession, at least in the following sense:

> ... the term Profession means an avocation whose activities are subjected to theoretical analysis, and are modified by theoretical conclusions derived from that analysis. This analysis has regard to the purposes of the avocation and to the adaptation of the activities for the attainment of those purposes. Such criticism (analysis) must be founded upon some understanding of the natures of things involved in those activities, so that the results of actions can be foreseen. *Thus foresight based upon theory, and theory based upon understanding of the nature of things, are essential to a profession.* (emphasis supplied).... The antithesis to a profession is an avocation based upon customary activities and modified by the trial and error of individual practice. Such an avocation is a craft, or at a lower level of individual skill it is merely a customary director of muscular labor.[13]

Whitehead recognizes that the distinction between crafts and professions is not always clear-cut. He also is one of the few writers to reject the popular assumption that professions have a monopoly on superior individuals. However, his somewhat unique definition places emphasis on the intellectual foundations of profession, and in this respect he is not alone.

The intellectual element of the profession idea is amply supported by generally accepted views on professional education. A profession is said to require a unified body of specialized knowledge which is built upon a

---

12. Those who stress practical applications seem anxious to exclude purely theoretical or abstract pursuits from profession status. However, it is not altogether clear whether they would deny profession status to learned persons who engage in scientific research, particularly theoretical research which leads or may lead to important practical applications. Distinctions between theoretical and practical pursuits can be so artificial that the distinctions themselves become unpractical and even useless.
13. Alfred North Whitehead, *Adventures of Ideas,* 1933, (New York: The Macmillan Company), pp. 72-73.

broad educational foundation.[14] Technical knowledge and skills are considered necessary, but they are not sufficient. They must be preceded by a solid background in the so-called "liberal" arts and sciences. The late Woodrow Wilson apparently went a step further, for he is credited with the remark: "The liberal education that our professional men get must not only be antecedent to their technical training; it must also be concurrent with it." In any case, the necessity of a broad general education is well established, as is the alternative formulation that professional education should be interdisciplinary in nature, i.e., it should stress the relationships among various disciplines or fields of thought. The need to understand such relationships is especially important to the "practice" of professions, since the *application* of knowledge and skills is unavoidably an interdisciplinary process.

Despite general acceptance of the professional's need for both specialized training and broad education, as well as agreement on the desirability of having the broad education come first in point of time, there is by no means a consensus on the proper mix or relative emphasis which should be placed upon the two types of preparation. This issue is not unique to the professions (educators are forever quarreling about the relative mix of liberal arts, science, and vocational subjects in nearly every curriculum). Nor is the issue one which can be divorced entirely from practical constraints such as time and money. To accommodate the need for a truly adequate base of liberal education and the pressures for more technical training, one can always make a theoretical case for lengthening the required period of preparation for a profession. But this would involve a corresponding increase in costs, and, if taken too far, the aspirants would be dead or nearing retirement age before they are "ready" to practice. The preparation time in medicine has lengthened, of course, along with the trend toward greater specialization.[15] In law, where the minimum preparation time has remained remarkably constant over the years, it is not yet clear whether the traditional resistance to recognizing subspecialties will continue. Nonetheless, the pressures toward longer minimum preparation times and more specialized train-

---

14. The virtually undisputed merits of this proposition are especially well expressed in the Overman monograph, op. cit., pp. 6-8.

15. Physicians also seem especially inclined to use the lengthy preparation time as a primary justification for high fees, usually on the theory that their large investment of time and money must be recovered over a shorter period of time — or at least justifies correspondingly large returns on the investment. The argument might be a little stronger if all physicians paid for their own schooling, but it fails to account for the relatively low incomes of history professors who may spend ten years earning doctoral degrees. Students of economics will recognize that demand, supply and other economic principles are needed to explain the distribution of income.

ing are already apparent in many occupational endeavors, including most of the recognized professions.[16] The nearly impossible task of trying to master everything inevitably forces at least some degree of specialization in our occupational pursuits, and it also helps explain the societal tendency to reserve the title "expert" for the specialist.

What persists is the nagging question of whether a specified blend of general education and specialized training sets professions apart from other occupations. Most definitions of profession ignore this issue. Their framers seem preoccupied with the existence of rigorous intellectual requirements, and they seem willing to accept as meeting this criterion a wide range of differences in the degree of difficulty, the relative emphasis on specialized knowledge, the relative emphasis as between the liberal arts and the sciences, and the length of the preparation time which is required as a precondition of the first level of practice. In point of fact, the range of accepted differences is wide enough to include many occupations which are not currently recognized as professions. Consequently, the intellectual ingredients of a profession have not been sharply defined, at least not beyond the consensus on the need for both liberal and technical preparation. Since as much can be said of nearly any occupation, is the real distinction that professions *require a minimum level* of intellectual preparation of all its practitioners? This cuts closer to the core of the matter, to be sure, yet it is not true of all members of all recognized professions (e.g., the clergy of some religions and religious denominations). It follows from the foregoing analysis that the intellectual requirements of profession do not alone establish its status. If they are to do so, they must be combined with other characteristics.

One should not lose sight of the overwhelming agreement on the need of professionals for *formal* preparation and study. Experience is necessary and potentially enriching, but it is not enough. Experience is at best a hard teacher. She gives the tests first and the lessons afterwards. At worst, she is no teacher at all. The latter point can be conveyed by the hackneyed notion that ten years of experience is often just one year of experience repeated ten times. Joseph Joubert said it more eloquently when he reminded us that "few men are worthy of experience; the majority let it corrupt them." It was the brilliant philosopher Kant, however, who left us with the wisdom of the following lines: "Thought without experience is empty; experience without thought is blind." Kant's message rings true after only a moment's reflection, does it not? It suggests, among other things, the futility of pretending that

---

16. Some observers are fearful that a trend away from specialized training might disqualify insurance from professional status. For example, see Patricia P. Douglas, "Professionalism: Its Presence and Absence in the Insurance Industry," *The Journal of Risk and Insurance,* Vol. XXXVIII, No. 2, June 1971, pp. 218-24.

thought and experience can be separated and ranked in importance. Neither has any real meaning or worth without the other. If only to give professions what Whitehead called "foresight based upon theory," experience must be complemented, supplemented and preceded by careful thought and study. To rely purely on trial-and-error is to reject the accumulated wisdom of previous generations. It is to repeat their mistakes. It is to invent the wheel over and over again. And, as if its inefficiency were not enough, its barriers to progress make the case. Thus it is that professional preparation demands more than experience.

There is also another important sense in which experience is not enough to justify an entitlement to profession status, for it is now widely accepted that admission to the ranks should be based upon proof of qualifications. The proof takes the form of passing the comprehensive examinations which are among the prerequisites to certification and/or licensure (along with prior experience requirements, in some cases). Such examinations are felt to be necessary and desirable for several reasons. Although there is always the potential danger that examinations can be used to impose unwarranted restrictions on entry to a profession, examinations can serve to (1) establish and preserve the status of a profession, (2) provide an equitable means to judge candidates or aspirants to the status, and (3) give uninitiated members of the lay public a meaningful way to distinguish between qualified and unqualified practitioners. Testing is an imperfect mechanism at best, but its advantages over other alternatives have been accepted, sometimes reluctantly, at almost every level of formal education. Examinations are used from elementary school on to determine our entitlement to proceed to the next level and our status as a graduate of prior levels. So also do we have university admissions exams, bar and medical exams, and the exams to measure entitlement to CPA, CPCU, CLU, and similar professional designations. At a minimum, the existence of such examinations imposes upon nonpassers and nontakers alike the entire burden of proving to the public that they are as qualified as persons who do pass the exams. Less perfectly, the various exams offer some help in defining the minimum standards to be met by professions. Very few still cling to the notion that a mere license to operate is reliable proof of professional preparation.[17] Most insist that a better form of proof lies in comprehen-

17. Milton Friedman, the Nobel Laureate, has made a convincing case against occupational licensure in Milton Friedman, *Capitalism And Freedom,* 1965 (The University of Chicago Press), Ch. IX. Friedman's engaging thesis is that the advantages claimed for occupational licensure are outweighed by the disadvantages, thus imposing unwarranted restrictions on individual freedom. Friedman is much more receptive to certification, however, if the certification is not done by the state and is not a precondition of practicing the occupation (a position which has been shared by the founding fathers of CPCU from the outset).

sive exams, experience requirements, and some kind of certification. Differences of opinion continue to arise, however, in determining which certifications or designations qualify their holders for profession status. While the existence of examinations and experience requirements does not assure profession status, and while experience requirements may not be as essential in the public's eye, the failure to meet the standards set by rigorous examinations seems a sure way of disqualifying occupations and individuals from the status they are seeking.

Mandatory Continuing Education

Until recently, the notion of *mandatory* continuing education has seldom been included in listings of the distinguishing characteristics of a profession.[18] The explanation is easy enough. Historically, in the United States at least, no recognized profession has ever *required* its members either to engage in continuing education or to provide tangible evidence of continuing competence. Nearly all professional associations and societies have urged upon their members the importance of maintaining and improving their professional knowledge and skills, and most have offered to their members a variety of continuing education programs and technical journals. Nonetheless, such programs frequently have not measured up to the rigor of the initial qualifying standards, and participation in them has nearly always been voluntary.

A dramatic shift in attitudes started to surface by the early 1970s, so much so that it is already safe to conclude, at this writing, that *mandatory* continuing education is an "idea whose time has come" for the professions. While the developments to date have been uneven among the established professions, the pattern which is beginning to take shape has all the earmarks of an unmistakable general trend. The study of these patterns has even motivated one writer to venture the more specific conclusion that "all professions are moving in the direction of recertification based on mandatory continuing education."[19] Most

---

18. For a notable exception, see Elmer G. Beamer, "Continuing Education—A Professional Requirement," *The Journal of Accountancy,* January 1972, pp. 33-39. For an excellent summary and analysis of mandatory education developments up to late 1975, see the October 1975 issue of the *Michigan State Bar Journal.* Almost the entire issue of this journal is devoted to a series of articles, some reprinted from other publications, on the continuing education approaches of the various recognized professions.

19. Douglas H. Parker, *Michigan State Bar Journal,* op. cit., at p. 794, in an article entitled "Periodic Recertification of Lawyers: A Comparative Study of Programs for Maintaining Professional Competence," reprinted from the *Utah Law Review,* Fall 1974, No. 3.

knowledgeable observers seem reluctant to accept recertification requirements as a clear-cut trend, but they do not deny the increasing momentum toward some kind of required demonstration of continuing professional competence.

Accounting, a comparative newcomer to profession status, merited the recognition by playing the leading role in implementing programs of mandatory continuing education. As of September 1974, fourteen states had adopted formal recertification programs requiring continuing education as a condition of the periodic renewal of a license to practice accounting.[20] Another state followed suit in 1975, and a dozen others were considering the matter.[21] By the fall of 1977, mandatory continuing education had become a condition of remaining in public accounting practice in twenty-two states.[22] Most of these requirements were imposed by specific laws enacted by the state legislatures, though a few take the form of state accountancy board regulations or amendments of state CPA society bylaws. It also should be noted that the vast majority of the remaining states have at least provided formal continuing education programs of a voluntary nature. And the pressures to make them compulsory seem destined to continue.

In accounting, the typical recertification and mandatory education program vests the implementation authority with the state board of accountancy. Accountants who are not engaged in public accounting are normally exempted. The board defines the various kinds of educational activities which will be acceptable, stipulates the number of hours to be completed over a specified time period, and has the power of suspension, revocation or nonrenewal of the licenses of those who do not comply. A typical approach is to require completion of 120 hours of acceptable continuing education activities during the three-year period immediately preceding the renewal date of the annual permit to practice accounting. Beyond these generalizations, no further summary will be

---

20. Ibid., p. 783.
21. Gordon S. May, "Continuing Professional Education — Required or Voluntary," *The Journal of Accountancy,* August 1975, p. 110-13. May's survey of fifty-four CPA societies showed that the continuing education programs mandated by the legislatures produced not only greater increases in attendance but also a higher degree of CPA satisfaction than the voluntary programs, though sharp increases in attendance were recorded for both voluntary and compulsory programs.
22. C. Dwayne Dowell and Wilton T. Anderson, "CPA Requirements of the States," *Collegiate News and Views,* Vol. XXXI, No. 1, Fall 1977. The article provides a list of the twenty-two states with continuing education requirements for accountants, as well as a state-by-state breakdown of the other CPA requirements.

attempted here, since the details of the programs vary from state to state.[23]

In the field of medicine, there have likewise been noteworthy movements toward continuing education requirements. A brief summary of these developments is made easier by first recognizing the existence of the following types of medical organization: state boards of medical examiners (which conduct examinations and *license* physicians to practice); national medical specialty boards (which conduct specialty examinations and *certify* physicians as specialists); state medical associations (which are private organizations somewhat like state bar associations); and, national specialty societies (which are also private organizations). Whereas the state boards are vested with the licensing authority, the national specialty boards have certification authority for specialists.

By 1974, four states had passed permissive legislation which authorized their state medical boards to impose continuing education requirements as a condition of license reregistration, and two states were in the process of doing so.[24] Seven state medical associations had adopted continuing education requirements as a condition of membership, along with two specialty societies (The American Academy of Family Physicians and the American Society of Abdominal Surgeons). Nearly all of the mandatory programs required a minimum of 150 hours of continuing education over a three-year period. In addition to the mandatory programs required for licensure or membership, voluntary continuing education programs were reported to have been attracting over 185,000 physicians annually. The scope of voluntary continuing education programs is suggested by the 1972 expenditure of over $10 million by the medical specialty societies alone!

One of the most interesting developments in medicine is the establishment of voluntary "self-assessment programs" by over a dozen of the medical societies, primarily the specialty societies. Under the typical self-assessment program, the participating physician completes a rigorous examination and returns it to a board of medical examiners. The exam is graded and returned to the physician, on a confidential basis, along with a grading key and a table which permits the physician to

23. The variations in the number of hours required are listed in C. Dwayne Dowell and Wilton T. Anderson, op. cit. By resolution, the AICPA Council promulgated continuing education guidelines and urged that they be adopted at the state level. These guidelines are contained in Elmer G. Beamer, op. cit., p. 36. The ethics code of the AICPA also imposes a broad continuing education obligation on all CPAs.
24. The information in this section was obtained from Douglas H. Parker, op. cit., Parker derived the data from a survey conducted by the American Medical Association's Department of Continuing Medical Education.

compare his or her performance with that of other participants. Many of the programs also supply the physician with an analysis of each question, a subject index, references for further study, and a reprint service for the references. Such programs have reportedly enjoyed widespread participation among the physician-members.

The "peer review" concept is also well established in medicine. In fact, with the passage of the Social Security Amendments of 1972, peer review of an elaborate nature is now mandated in connection with all compensable services rendered under medicare and medicaid. Peer review has long been important to the many physicians who desire and need to practice in hospitals, however, because the entitlement to practice in a hospital is controlled by a staff credentials committee, which further determines the scope of a physician's hospital privileges by establishing different classes of staff membership.

In accounting, peer review was first mandated by the Securities and Exchange Commission in the handling of several disciplinary cases. Then, in 1974, the American Institute of Certified Public Accountants (AICPA) adopted a voluntary peer review program for a review of the operations and procedures of large, multioffice accounting firms.

In the field of college teaching, peer review and mandatory continuing education have had an historical role which seems to be increasing in importance in many (if not most) universities. True, there is often more weight given to research and publications than to other evidence of teaching effectiveness, but the career of a typical college professor invariably involves several types of continuing evaluation. For example, the various accreditation agencies evaluate the professional credentials of individual faculty members and use these evaluations in determining whether a college or university is to obtain or lose its accreditation status. More directly, faculty members are regularly evaluated by deans, department chairpersons and committees of faculty peers, for the purpose of determining pay raises, rank promotions, tenure status and reappointment contracts or dismissals. While tenured faculty members are very seldom dismissed on the grounds of a failure to engage in *formal* continuing education programs per se, they can be dismissed for dereliction of duties or gross incompetence (though as a practical matter it is not often done).[25] Tenured faculty also share with nontenured faculty a vulnerability to pay "freezes" for failure to meet the required standards

---

25. This author freely acknowledges a strong bias against the current concept of faculty tenure. However, there is some consolation in knowing that the better universities do not hand out tenure freely, and lesser universities are making concerted efforts to toughen the requirements for tenure status. In fairness to colleagues, one should also confess that the case for some kind of tenure is not without merit. But the subject is too complex to deal with adequately in the limited space available.

of professional growth and development. And all faculty members are required to have specified educational degrees as a precondition of rank. University faculty appointments, ranked from lowest to highest, are as follows: instructor or lecturer; Assistant Professor; Associate Professor; and Full Professor, the highest rank obtainable (except for largely honorary titles like "Distinguished Professor" or "Chairholder"). Universities do appoint a limited number of instructors who have only baccalaureate or masters degrees, but accreditation agencies require that a large proportion of the total faculty must have "terminal" degrees in their respective fields (normally a doctorate). Moreover, very few universities will grant even the Assistant Professor rank to persons who do not have the doctorate degree as a precondition, and fewer still will grant such persons any rank above the Assistant Professor level. A number of colleges of business require, or give preferential treatment to, persons who also hold the CPCU, CLU, or CPA professional designations. One should likewise acknowledge that universities are making increasing use of unsigned questionnaires and other formal devices through which faculty members are evaluated by their students. Teaching is a very visible field, in the sense that incompetence does not pass unnoticed by students. Students are not reluctant to criticize, if doing so does not affect their grades, and they demand standards of performance of the type and degree to which practitioners of other occupations are not always subjected. Though some observers are encouraged by occasional signs of progress, there is still a long way to go toward the establishment and maintenance of more meaningful professional standards for college and university teachers.[26]

The field of law has lagged even further behind accounting and medicine in the development and implementation of mandatory continuing education programs, a fact of life which is embarrassing to no small portion of the legal profession. The maintenance-of-competence requirements for law school professors are broadly similar to those just described for other college teachers.[27] In the case of practicing attorneys, formalized peer review, self-assessment examinations and mandatory

---

26. Elementary and secondary teachers must meet continuing education requirements in a number of states. They probably feel they have a long way to go, too, for they are not insulated from the internal pressures of pride or the external pressures of a more demanding public.

27. In the ivory towers of university life, critics of legal education are sometimes disturbed by the large number of law faculty who do not have any earned degrees beyond the LL.B. (Bachelor of Laws). Such critics are not satisfied by the fact that some law schools have replaced the LL.B. with an LL.D. (Doctor of Laws) or a J.D. (Doctor of Jurisprudence or Doctor of Laws), since the change of degrees is often effected without any corresponding change in the educational requirements.

continuing education programs are widely discussed and advocated in the legal journals and the bar associations. However, as late as 1975, the primary action had been limited to the ruling of one state's supreme court. The Supreme Court of Minnesota adopted rules requiring continuing legal education compliance as a prerequisite to the right to continue the practice of law.[28] Briefly, the Minnesota rules establish a State Board of Continuing Legal Education, appointed by the Court, and stipulate that an attorney who desires to maintain "active status" must provide satisfactory proof that he or she has completed, over the previous three-year period, a minimum of forty-five hours of approved course work, either as a student or a lecturer. Attorneys who desire "restricted status" are exempted from the mandatory continuing education and compliance certification provisions, but they cannot (within Minnesota) represent any person on legal matters, other than a close relative or a full-time employer.

It is hard to tell whether the Minnesota continuing education rules have established a pattern for the legal profession at large. The important developments in other states have been fairly recent and rapid, and monitoring them would be a formidable undertaking. Conceivably, programs designed to maintain the competence of practicing attorneys could be implemented by the bar associations, but meaningful programs of a mandatory nature would be difficult to impose, as a practical matter, because the sanction of expulsion from membership in a "nonintegrated" bar association would be of little consequence to many attorneys; it does not affect their license to practice law.[29] Mandatory programs established by the highest court in each state may have a better chance of succeeding, therefore, in that such courts have the power to impose educational requirements as a condition of maintaining the right to practice law. Such requirements might also be imposed (by the particular court or governmental body, in each case) on the narrower right to practice law before the federal courts, the SEC and/or the United States Patent Office. It is likewise conceivable that law may be forced to recognize and certify a number of additional subspecialties within the field.[30] The case for specialization appears to be just as strong in law as it

---

28. "First Interim Report on Mandatory Continuing Legal Education," Committee on Continuing Legal Education, State Bar of Michigan, *Michigan State Bar Journal,* op. cit., pp. 762-67. The relevant rules of the Supreme Court of Minnesota are attached as an addendum to the committee's report.

29. Douglas H. Parker, *Michigan State Bar Journal,* op. cit., pp. 770-71.

30. Specialization has been permitted in the historically recognized specialties of admiralty, trademark and patent law. California has adopted specialty programs in criminal law, workers' compensation and taxation. Many lawyers tend to specialize anyway, apart from whether the specialty is officially recognized by the bar.

is in medicine, and it is not unrelated to the matter of maintaining the competence of practicing attorneys. In any event, a vocal portion of the legal fraternity has not been wildly enthusiastic about the notions of specialization, peer review, self-assessment exams or formalized continuing education requirements. It will likely take some time for a clear-cut pattern to emerge.

Although time and space limitations do not permit the luxury of exploring the important developments in other occupational fields, perhaps the sampling has been enough to demonstrate that professions are feeling the mounting pressures to adopt some kind of mandatory continuing education programs. What are the sources of these pressures? Some have attributed the pressures partly to an intensified social consciousness and the increasing demands made by clients and patients. Most people probably know little or nothing about the existence or absence of mandatory continuing education in the professions, but many persons do tend to seek out the experts, whenever they have a choice, and such persons would undoubtedly prefer some sort of tangible evidence that a professional is "current" in his or her field. There is likewise merit in the argument that the conscience of many professionals has evolved into a tardy realization that their professional competence can become quickly outdated by the rapid changes and increasing complexity of their fields. But the potential gap between initial competence and continuing competence is hardly a new phenomenon. Hence, it could well be that the growing social consciousness of professionals has been sparked as much by the desire to maintain their professional status, alongside the professions which are moving toward mandatory continuing education, and by a fear that the failure to take the initiative will prompt government action to fill the void. Realistically, no mandatory continuing education program will be completely successful in weeding out all the incompetents in a profession, yet the failure to try may ultimately be the very thing which will disqualify some groups from profession status. If so, it is time to accept mandatory continuing education as a central characteristic of the profession concept.

A Formal Association or Society

The greater number of observers treat the existence of formal associations or societies as an essential characteristic of professions, whether the associations are at several levels or at the national level alone. Proponents point to the need for a unified and cohesive group to set ethical standards and provide continuing education programs and publications for its members or "alumni," as they are sometimes referred to in less formal terms. These worthy goals are best achieved, proponents feel, through elected leaders, an adequate professional staff, adequate financial resources, and the power of many persons working together toward common objectives and shared interests.

One can fully accept the validity and beneficial aspects of professional societies without overlooking that the power to do good is also the power to do evil. The associations and societies of some established professions have used their powers to impose questionable restrictions on entry into the profession, as well as to sanctify protectionism and other self-serving objectives which may not be in the *public* interest. To that extent, they have lost hold of their claims to altruism.

In a definitional sense, the necessity of a formal association is logically derived from the presupposition that profession is a collective or group concept. If one profession is to be distinguished from other professions and occupational groupings, it must have the kind of identity which only becomes visible in a formal organization. This conclusion is not necessarily contradicted by the splintering of medicine into subspecialties. While physicians do not constitute a completely homogeneous group, physicians (as a group) are distinguishable from other professions and occupational groups. However, a group having a very heterogeneous composition may be indistinguishable from other groups, or it may lump members who meet the tests of profession with members who do not. The latter helps explain why it might be less than convincing to treat accounting or insurance as professions per se. It also helps account for the occasional argument in support of treating insurance agents and/or brokers and consultants as a subgroup more worthy of profession status (assuming they have met the other tests), since their representation of clients makes them more like practicing attorneys and physicians than it does, say, home office underwriters. Whether the reader or author accepts this particular view is beside the point. It is presented here merely to underscore that the struggle to find identity and purpose in a profession is a struggle for which most individuals want the assistance of a strong group. In each of the recognized professions there is a satisfying sense of fraternity or "brotherhood" which is a natural result of bringing together individuals who share common interests, problems, goals, and educational backgrounds, and who speak in the language of an esoteric technical jargon that is seldom understood outside their numbers. When this sense of fraternity is diminished by a growing diversity within the membership, the pressures to form subgroups may conflict with the desire to retain the greater strength of a larger group. In any case, the existence of associations and societies is a necessary part of giving the group a distinct identity.

Independence

Group action may be required for some purposes. It does not relieve the professional from the burden of making individual judgments. To serve the needs of those whom it is the professional's duty or privilege to serve on a daily basis, the professional must be free to exercise sound professional judgment and skill. The scholar needs academic freedom, the airline pilot needs the authority to make quick decisions, and all professionals need to be free from monetary or other external influences which inherently impair the exercise of sound judgment and skill. But no freedom can be absolute. The professional who does not operate within ethical and legal boundaries is exposed to the risks of departure. The physician is a willing captive of his own religious views on abortion. And mistakes in judgment will be made.

Though one sometimes yearns for the tiller scales of justice to be equipped with the red tilt light of a pinball game, or a machine which would instantly prescribe the proper treatment for medical ills, or an electronic device which would replace baseball umpires in the calling of balls and strikes, even the best physicians and lawyers are as capable of errors in judgment as the worst baseball umpires. The difference between them lies in the gravity of consequences they may inflict upon others. The prudent professional will be mindful of his limitations, therefore, and will often seek the advice and counsel of peers or superiors. But the latter are illustrations of sound judgment, not substitutes for it. They cannot totally relieve the professional of the laboring oar of individual judgment. Accordingly, "independence" may be thought of as a distinguishing characteristic of a profession.

In public accounting, the notion of independence has a strikingly different purpose than it does in law and medicine. The professional standards of the American Institute of Certified Public Accountants (AICPA) embrace "independence, integrity and objectivity" as affirmative ethical principles, and they stipulate that "independence has always been a concept fundamental to the accounting profession, the cornerstone of its philosophical structure."[31] Independence is defined by the accounting profession as "the ability to act with integrity and objectivity." However, it should be stressed that a CPA who is engaged in the practice of public accounting is expected to be independent *of those he serves* (emphasis supplied). Why should CPAs be independent from their clients? If CPAs do not maintain their independence from clients, their professional opinions on financial statements will be of little value to

---

31. *AICPA Professional Standards,* Vol. 2, 1976, published for the American Institute of Certified Public Accountants by Commerce Clearing House, Inc., pp. 4282 and 4291.

creditors, investors, government agencies, and others who rely upon such statements, including clients. It follows that independence, as well as competence, is essential to the profession status of public accounting.

A decidedly different standard of independence is applied to the practice of law, where an undivided loyalty is said to be owed to the client. The American Bar Association's revised Code of Professional Responsibility stipulates, in Canon 5, that "A lawyer should exercise independent professional judgment on behalf of a client."[32] This broad concept is further clarified in twenty-four related guidelines, illustrative of which is the following:

> EC 5-1 The professional judgment of a lawyer should be exercised, within the bounds of the law, *solely for the benefit of his client* and free of compromising influences and loyalties. Neither his personal interests, the interests of other clients, *nor the desires of third persons should be permitted to dilute his loyalty to his client.* (emphasis supplied)[33]

Critics of the legal profession do not question the lawyer's need for freedom to make independent professional judgments. What they do challenge is the lawyer's ethical obligation to exercise that judgment solely for the benefit of his client, particularly in situations where an undivided loyalty to the client's interests would not be, or might not be, in the *public* interest. This criticism is implicit in the popular concern about the ethical propriety of lawyers using fine legal procedures and technicalities to free persons who would otherwise be convicted of serious crimes. Criminal defense attorneys are quick to interpose the counter-argument that the most vigorous possible defense of every accused is ultimately in the public interest. Since the counter-argument has philosophical merits which thoughtful persons do not dismiss lightly, it could be that some critics are shooting at the wrong target. That is to say, the critics seem to be wanting lawyers to observe (what are perceived as) "higher" ethical standards than the law requires. Perhaps what they really want, as respects criminal law, is for the courts and legislatures to redefine the "public interest," in part by imposing narrower legal boundaries on the lawyer's freedom to exercise

---

32. *Code of Professional Responsibility,* adopted by the House of Delegates of the American Bar Association in 1969 and amended in 1970. The Code, which was adopted by the Supreme Court of Pennsylvania in 1970, is included in a 1974 publication of the Pennsylvania Bar Association. In the latter publication, Canon 5 and its related "ethical considerations" and "disciplinary rules" are found on pp. 18-23. The page references would differ in the various other publications which contain the ABA Code.

33. Ibid, p. 18. The guidelines are referred to as "ethical considerations," and they are translated into more specific "disciplinary rules" of a binding nature.

independent judgment on behalf of an accused client. If this were to be done, the lawyer would still be ethically obligated to give undivided loyalty to the client and to stay within the bounds of law, but the narrower legal boundaries would leave less room for individual judgment in defining the public interest. However, given the outside legal boundaries at any time, it is hard to establish that a lawyer's vigorous defense of a client is contrary to the public interest just because it is based on seemingly minor technicalities, since the courts and the legislatures, by permitting the technicalities, have in that sense defined the public interest.

Critics of the lawyer's undivided loyalty to a client may have a slightly stronger case in the context of corporate law. For instance, the ABA's Code of Professional Responsibility contains the following ethical consideration:

> EC 5-18   A lawyer employed or retained by a corporation or similar entity owes his allegiance to the entity and not to a stockholder, director, officer, employee, representative, or other person connected with the entity. In advising the entity, a lawyer should keep paramount its interests and his professional judgment should not be influenced by . . . the personal desires of any person or organization . . . .[34]

In the light of these and other relevant provisions in the ABA Code, it is not altogether clear whether the practicing attorney has an ethical obligation to serve a corporate client's interests in situations where the client's interests would conflict with those of employees, creditors, stockholders, government agencies, or others who rely upon the corporation's integrity. It is certainly made explicit that the attorney is expected to operate within the boundaries of law, that he may refuse to represent a corporate client, and that he may be ethically required to withdraw from such representation under various specified circumstances. But once the lawyer accepts a corporate client, as long as his conduct is neither illegal nor otherwise contrary to a specific ethics rule, his undivided loyalty to the corporate client apparently *permits* him (and may even *require* him) to serve various clients' interests which may conflict with the interests of others. If an attorney were not permitted to do so, of course, he or she would not be able to represent corporate clients in matters of litigation. Nonetheless, it is unmistakably clear that the professional independence standards which govern lawyers are quite different from those governing public accountants. Whereas the practicing lawyer's obligation of independence is aimed at fostering and enhancing his advocacy *for* his client, the public accountant's independence is an independence *from* his client, so that the accountant's pro-

---

34. Ibid., p. 20.

fessional opinions may also serve the interests of others who rely upon them.

The general idea of independence is also a characteristic of the medical profession; yet it appears in several different forms, and the practicing physician is given considerable latitude in their application. The point is most easily illustrated by referring to the American Medical Association's "Principles of Medical Ethics," which are broadly applicable to all practicing physicians.[35] Section one of these principles sets the tone, by stipulating that "the principal objective of the medical profession is to render service to humanity with full respect for the dignity of man," and by further noting that physicians should render to each of their patients "a full measure of service and devotion." Various other sections admonish the physician to obey all laws and to render his services in emergency situations; otherwise, the physician is free to choose whom he will serve, short of soliciting patients. Section six also deals with the notion of independence, in the following way:

> A physician should not dispose of his services under terms or conditions which tend to interfere with or impair the free and complete exercise of his medical judgment and skill or tend to cause a deterioration of the quality of medical care.

A physician is free, under section seven, to charge a fee which is "commensurate with the services rendered and the patient's ability to pay," and to dispense "drugs, remedies or appliances" when doing so "is in the best interests of the patient." However, an additional limit on the physician's independence is apparent in the section eight admonition that "a physician should seek consultation upon request; in doubtful or difficult cases; or whenever it appears that the quality of medical service may be enhanced thereby." Furthermore, a physician is not quite as free to protect confidential information as many people seem to believe. The relevant section of the ethical principles, section nine, is as follows:

> A physician may not reveal the confidences intrusted to him in the course of medical attendance, or the deficiencies he may observe in the character of patients, unless he is required to do so by law *or unless it becomes necessary in order to protect the welfare of the individual or the community.* (emphasis supplied)

---

35. "Principles of Medical Ethics," 1974 printing, The American Medical Association, Chicago, Illinois. The preamble makes it clear that these principles are in the nature of general guidelines rather than binding rules. Moreover, as noted earlier, the AMA per se could do little more than expel a violator from membership, even if they were binding rules, since licensure is regulated by state boards of medical examiners and specialty certification is controlled by national medical specialty boards.

The net effect of the various ethical principles is too complex to capture in a simple description. In fact, perhaps the only safe conclusion is that a physician's independence is tempered by a number of ethical and legal constraints, within which the physician is given considerable freedom to exercise his professional judgment. Most of the ethical constraints appear to be motivated by a desire to preserve or enhance the quality of medical care rendered to patients, while a few appear to be motivated by a desire to serve a larger public interest (e.g., the ethical obligation to provide emergency treatment and the obligation to disclose confidential information to protect the welfare of the community). What emerges, in any case, is an overall concept of independence which is somewhat unique to the medical profession.

Despite the different standards of independence in public accounting, law, and medicine, many observers have preferred to stress two ways in which these professionals are ostensibly similar. Their practitioners have clients (or patients), and the practitioners are compensated on a fee-for-service basis.

Those who stress the necessity of a client or patient relationship would deny profession status to occupations which do not involve direct service to individual members of the public. By extension of their own argument, they would be forced to deny profession status to the many competent and ethical lawyers, physicians, and CPAs who are salaried employees of one employer, rather than engaged in "public practice" per se (and they would be stretching a point if they did not exclude many members of the clergy and physicians engaged solely in medical research). Actuaries would be engaged in a profession only if they were consulting actuaries, and so on, until the field is narrowed to the "chosen few" with profession status. The merits of this argument are not apparent to the writer. What is more, the argument skirts the issue of independence, for it is entirely possible to engage in a public practice for individual clients without any measure of professional independence, and it is actually quite common for salaried employees of one employer to enjoy a large measure of professional independence and freedom to make judgments (e.g., college professors).

The fee-for-service basis of compensation gets closer to an important characteristic shared by public accounting, law, and medicine, but its importance is derived from its consistency with the different types of independence which each profession is ethically obligated to exercise. The ultimate goal of the professions is to maintain and improve the quality of services rendered to those whom it is the professional's duty or privilege to serve. Achieving this goal requires not only technical competence and ethical attitudes among professionals; it also requires that professionals have the independence or freedom to make sound professional judgments, to apply their knowledge and skills, unselfishly, in ways which will best serve the needs of others. The basis of compensation is but one of several means of fostering the required types of independence. While most of the established professions make use of the fee-for-service basis of compensation, they also make use of other systems of compensation, and they rely on ethics standards to establish and control the kinds of independence they regard as important. Thus, a distinguishable degree of independence is the characteristic which recognized professions really have in common.

Unavoidably, the foregoing analysis summons a brief consideration of the perennial controversy among proponents of fees, commissions, or fee-commission offsets as the "proper" basis of compensating insurance agents and brokers. Most readers of this essay will not need to be told that the statutes and regulations of a number of jurisdictions continue to prohibit or restrict the charging of fees by those who represent insurance buyers and/or sellers. Nonetheless, by assuming that the pertinent laws and regulations could be changed, and by avoiding the temptation to delve into other arguments which might lead the discussion astray, one can concentrate on the specific issue of whether the prevailing compensation system is a barrier to profession status for insurance agents and brokers. One of the first to suggest this issue was the late Dr. C. A. Kulp, then Dean of the Wharton School of Finance and Commerce, who often made the following observation: "As long as the insurance agent continues to receive his compensation from the seller and not the buyer, one important element of professionalism will be missing." Some immediately jumped to the premature conclusion that Dr. Kulp was making a superficial brief against the entire commission system. Others, including those of us who were made to understand his purposes, realized that Kulp's primary teaching mission was to stimulate careful thought and reflection. In any event, a lot of very thoughtful people have since taken up the cause of demonstrating a link between the fee system and profession status. And some have insisted that the fee system is a *prerequisite* to profession status for insurance practitioners.[36]

The usual argument presupposes that if the true professional is to serve the needs of clients, he or she must have the kind of financial detachment which is permitted only by the fee-for-service basis of com-

---

36. For example, see William Peet, "Insurance—Present or Potential Profession," *CPCU Annals,* Vol. 13, No. 2, Fall 1960, pp. 165-72. See also Peet's follow-up communication, "A Profession for CPCUs," *CPCU Annals,* Vol. 16, No. 1, Spring 1963, pp. 82-87. For a scholarly look at the fee vs. commissions controversy, an analysis of the legal restrictions and proposed solutions, see E.J. Leverett, Jr. and James S. Trieschmann, "Fees vs. Commissions: Are They Legal?" *CPCU Annals,* Vol. 27, No. 4, December 1974, pp. 266-70.

pensation. Since the fee is charged, regardless of whether the advice is taken, the compensation basis does not unduly influence the nature of the advice. The advisor, having been freed from the temptation to structure the advice solely in a way which would maximize his own financial returns, can concentrate on an objective analysis of the client's needs. The commission-only system provides strong incentives for the wrong kind of self-serving advice, it is argued, because the advisor's income is based entirely on a percentage of the total number of premium dollars he or she can generate. Large premium dollars bring large incomes to producers, whereas zero premium dollars offer nothing but the hope of a future sale. Consequently, some insurance policyholders or prospective buyers get little or no advice, some pay too much for insurance coverages which meet their needs, and some end up with the wrong kinds of coverage. Such results can be attributed largely to a lack of knowledge and skills among numerous insurance producers *and* buyers, as well as to the questionable ethics of a portion of both groups. But proponents of the fee system cling to the idea that the commission-only system is a major barrier to professionalism, at least in the minds of the general public. Highly competent and ethical producers must face the practical implications of giving free advice. And skeptical buyers, aware that the producer's income depends upon a sale, are quite reluctant to follow even the best advice, perhaps especially if it is given free of charge.

The obvious merits of such arguments are received with varying degrees of enthusiasm in the community of sophisticated corporate insurance buyers. Some do favor the fee system, for the general reasons already noted. Others would prefer a fee-commission offset system, under the terms of which a producer would be free to charge a fee for consulting services rendered. If the corporation places some of the recommended insurance through the producer, and the commission is larger than the fee, the commission is accepted as full payment for the producer's services, with no additional cost to the buyer. If the commission on the insurance is less than the fee, the buyer is billed for the difference. Some corporate insurance buyers also favor a sliding-scale commission system of the kind which has long been used in group life insurance, i.e., a system where the commission *rate* declines with higher levels of premium volume (in other words, the rate of commission varies inversely with premium volume). Still other corporate insurance buyers are indifferent about which compensation system is used. Sophisticated buyers will get what is best for the corporation under any of the producer compensation systems, according to this rationale, because knowledgeable buyers know what the fee or commission will be, and they will not allow the producer's compensation to get out of line with the quantity and quality of services the producer actually provides.

That it is far easier to be ethical without any temptations to be unethical is axiomatic. However, if public opinion gives profession status to some occupations and denies it to insurance producers because of the commission system, it could be that the public is less aware of quite similar systems among the established professions. For example, it is common practice to compensate hospital pathologists with a percentage of the gross pathology charges of the hospital (35 percent in one hospital for which this author sat on a budget review committee). This approach obviously provides incentives for higher pathology rates and the ordering of unnecessary diagnostic tests, particularly now that "defensive medicine" is a widely used safeguard against malpractice claims. Yet, abuse can be minimized by the ethics of the pathologist, efficient hospital administration, hospital review boards, peer review, insurance companies, and government agencies. Less controllable is the office practice of many general practitioners and medical specialists. Most rely heavily on fees (and insurance to pay them) and the overwhelming demand for their services. Some increase their hourly rates to maintain the desired gross income and keep the demand for their services at a manageable level. Many will accept no new patients. But some continue to charge a flat rate per patient or varying flat rates for different types of service; and, as the jam-packed waiting rooms of physicians' quarters will confirm, their incomes can be increased or maintained only if they see a certain number of patients each day. Their incomes are just about as closely linked to "production" or volume as the insurance producer's, and this can lead to a deterioration in the quality of medical service they provide each patient. Attracting physician-partners to ease the load is very difficult in less desirable communities, which in turn leaves the physician with an ethical choice that the majority of insurance producers may never have to make. Faced with excessive demand for his or her services, the physician must decide whether to see more patients and spend less time with each, increase the number of working hours at the risk of the physician's own health, turn away patients who want and seriously need medical attention, or some combination thereof, even if total income is not a primary factor in making the decision.

Practicing ophthalmologists sometimes derive no small portion of their incomes from ownership interests in optical businesses situated on or near the premises, a sort of "locational quasi-monopoly." The compensation of law and medical partners is often related, respectively, to the volume of law business they generate or the amount of surgery they perform. Every recognized profession has its share of book authors who receive substantial percentage royalties (a noble word for commissions) on the sales volume. Every recognized profession has a large share of members who participate in profit-sharing plans financed from the profits of their own practice. Plaintiffs' attorneys take a percentage of dollar amounts they recover for clients and call the commission a "contingent fee." And these are just a *few* illustrations of professional compensation arrangements which are not fundamentally different, in terms of their potential effect, from the commission system for insurance producers. Sure, one could pick at the illustrations by observing that some of them do involve percentage payments of a seller directly to an intermediary, or that an author does not normally peddle his own books. The shortcomings of the analogies do not alter the basic point, however, about the variety of compensation arrangements used by established professions. Nearly all of these arrangements, including hourly fees, offer strong financial incentives for the professional to do some very unprofessional things, and each of the recognized professions has its share of members who succumb to the temptations. There are surgeons who perform totally unnecessary surgery, pathologists who order unnecessary tests, lawyers who "chase ambulances," accountants who falsify financial statements, teachers who take bribes for good grades. Would such persons be any more inclined to do these things if the money came in an envelope stamped "commission from the seller?" Would insurance producers automatically enjoy profession status if they, like physicians, were ethically obligated to charge the client a fee based on his ability to pay?

Members of the general public are probably not aware of the full extent to which established professions make use of commission-type compensation arrangements, whereas they are aware that insurance producers are compensated by commissions. Furthermore, most insurance buyers are well aware of the fact that the requirements for an agent's or broker's license are quite minimal compared to the extensive time, education, and testing required to practice law or medicine. They likewise perceive some sharp differences in the kinds of ethical standards which are applicable to practicing insurance producers, lawyers, and physicians. A physician who overtly solicits individual patients is known to be violating explicit ethical standards; an insurance producer who solicits customers is known to be doing what is expected of a producer. Physicians are ethically obligated to expose quacks among their numbers, and they should bring pressure to revoke the quack's license to practice medicine. Insurance agents and brokers are seldom under any explicit ethical obligation to expose "quackery" within their ranks, and few bother to try, unless it has affected them directly (e.g., where an agent loses a life insurance policy because of the statutory "twisting" of a competitor). Indeed, some producers seem to look upon "squealers" with contempt; or, they at least prefer to govern their own conduct by the unwritten ethic of "mind your own business," leaving it largely up to the regulatory authorities to discover incompetence or

wrongdoing. Public perceptions of *all* producers are also tainted, undoubtedly, by the conduct of overly-aggressive insurance salespersons
(where their impact on public perceptions has overshadowed their numbers). Thus, while it could be that the public would like to take away the
profession status of the pathologist who gets a percentage cut of the
hospital's gross pathology charges, it seems more likely that the commission system of insurance producers is a secondary issue in the public's eye. To further dramatize the point, let us make the *highly* unrealis-
tic and *untrue assumption* that the insurance producer group eventually
became composed entirely of high school dropouts who operate under no
ethical or legal constraints, solicit customers aggressively, and charge
each customer an hourly fee for services rendered. Would they now
qualify for profession status? Conversely, if all producers could demonstrate mastery of knowledge and skills and adherence to very high
ethical standards, would a commission basis of compensation deny them
profession status in the public eye? One cannot be sure. One only
suspects.

The foregoing discussion is not intended to be an argument in support of either commissions or fees. It will instead suggest why *independence,* not compensation per se, may play a more crucial role in the
concept of a profession. The importance of professional independence
was expressed succinctly by the Committee on Ethics of the American
Psychiatric Association when, in speaking of a particular type of contractual arrangement, it said:

> The ethical question is not the contract itself but whether or not the
> physician is free of unnecessary nonmedical interference. *The ulti-
> mate issue is the freedom to offer good quality medical care.* (em-
> phasis supplied)[37]

The kinds of independence a professional needs (and does not need) have
been fairly well defined in public accounting, law, and medicine, mostly
by their written codes of ethics. However, the nature of the independence required by insurance producers remains controversial, vague
and essentially undefined.

If the insurance producer is to be free to offer the best quality of
"insurance care" to clients, does this require the insurance producer to
be an "independent" agent or broker in the insurance sense of the term?
Does an agent who represents one insurance company exclusively have
sufficient professional independence? Does either the exclusive agent or
the independent agent have sufficient control over the supply of insurance or the quality of insurance contracts and insurer services? Would a

---

37. "The Principles of Medical Ethics with Annotations Especially Applicable
to Psychiatry," *American Journal of Psychiatry,* 130:9, September 1973,
p. 1062.

fee system of compensation give the producer better control over the supply of insurance or the quality of insurance contracts or the quality of insurer services? Glib answers to such questions may continue to pose barriers to profession status and progress.

For a variety of reasons, the independence models of medicine, law, and public accounting may not be completely transplantable for the insurance producer. With the partial exception of medicine and drugs, the physician is not an intermediary for a company or companies, and he has direct and substantial control over the supply and quality of health care rendered to his patients. Maybe some producers could charge fees for writing "insurance prescriptions," but the absence of a counterpart for local drugstores would require buyers to find purchasing agents, unless the producer also served as the pharmacist. If the advocacy role of a practicing attorney were to be emulated as a model of independence, the producer would have to be a broker with undivided loyalty to the client he represents, and he probably would have to charge fees for his services.[38] However, the independence model of CPAs offers some interesting insights which have scarcely been mentioned in insurance publications. The ethical standards applicable to CPAs, remember, require them to be independent *from their clients,* so that they may serve the best interests of creditors, stockholders, and others who rely upon their professional opinions, including clients. There are interesting parallels here to the kind of independence which insurance producers truly need. For example, just as creditors, stockholders, and outsiders rely upon CPA opinions, so also do these same parties rely, consciously or otherwise, on the insurance recommendations of the producer. In fact, the same can be said of all third-party "beneficiaries" of insurance. The injured claimant relies upon liability insurance, the injured worker on compensation insurance, the spouse and children on life insurance, the mortgagee on fire insurance, the importer on ocean marine insurance, and even the hospital relies on the health insurance of its patients. In each case, the insurance producer is serving the insurance needs of others, as well as his clients. Maybe commissions are a necessary incentive for that reason alone (perhaps especially in life insurance, where most people need to be motivated to buy). But commissions may serve less effectively than fees to provide the producer with independence *from* his client. And so the web of complexity is spun.

The reality is that one currently finds aspects of various models of independence among insurance producers. In this respect, they are not

---

38. For a scholarly analysis by an experienced CPCU-lawyer who is highly respected by his fellow CPCUs, including this writer, see Robert M. Morrison, "The Anomalous Position of the Insurance Agent—An Invitation to Schizophrenia," *Villanova Law Review,* Spring 1967, pp. 535-44.

as homogeneous as the recognized professions. Whether the homogeneity of independence which might merit profession status would be a better servant of mankind than the current diversity of approaches is a question which deserves careful and deliberate study. Get on with it, CPCU candidates! The future is yours to mold.

Public Recognition as a Profession

Students of the profession concept have placed a considerable amount of emphasis on the matter of public recognition. Surprisingly, the very notion they are trying to emphasize is almost never defined. The pronounced tendency of writers to avoid the meaning of "public" implies a contentment with the use of weasel words like "general public," "public opinion," the "public as a whole," or the "public at large," so as to permit them to get on with the business of advocating a particular role of the public in distinguishing a profession.

There are undoubtedly situations and purposes for which casual references to the general public provide an acceptable convenience of language. The preceding pages contain many such references, to be sure. However, where the objective is to understand a position on the role of public opinion, it would be helpful to know whether its advocates are thinking about the opinions of a substantial majority of the entire U.S. population, a simple majority, a majority of adults, a plurality, or some other measure of opinion. At this level of specificity, the various advocates may have very different measures in mind. They obviously do not feel that profession status is conferred by a vote of Congress or by a 5 to 4 decision of the U.S. Supreme Court. They have a larger public in mind, and they may not be thinking of anything more specific than their own intuitive feelings about what portion of the population determines such things as profession status.

The writers are united in the belief that profession status comes gradually to its aspirants, if at all, and that shifts in public opinion can change the list of occupations which qualify. Yet, once again, they stop short of raising or addressing several troublesome issues. For instance, is the lay public really able to confer social status? Ordinary persons have little more than a remote and indirect influence on the matter of who is accepted in "high society" and put on the social register. Those who *confer* such social status are the people who already have it, and the conferees may or may not be popular choices or admired, either within the group of previous initiates or by members of the lay public who have not been accepted into the fold. Therefore, is it not conceivable that *profession* status may be conferred in a similar way?

Among the people who are not in the recognized professions, a majority or a vocal minority may greatly influence those who are in positions of power. The "non-profession" people are also perfectly free to view any occupation with admiration, indifference, or contempt, whether or not it is a recognized profession. They may aspire to become business executives, lawyers, or physicians, for whatever reasons they may have, and they may seek profession status for a previously unrecognized occupation. Nevertheless, members of the established professions probably will have the final say on which occupations are admitted. Or, to put it another way, aspirants of profession status would hardly be satisfied if their occupations were not recognized as professions by those who already hold the distinction. Aspirants would like to be thought of as professionals by everyone, no doubt, especially by clients, but acceptance by nonprofessionals would not be enough. It would have all the emptiness of knowing that everyone believes you are a great athlete, except the great athletes.

In the ebb and flow of published materials on the subject, one finds a wide range of opinion concerning the impact of "the" public (i.e., whichever public each author has in mind) on the idea of a profession. Some writers treat public acceptance as but one of several characteristics of a profession, while others see it as the only characteristic or the only one which truly matters. Seemingly, the weight of authority supports the view that public recognition of profession status is important, yet it is based upon whether an occupation adequately meets various criteria. The latter view is well illustrated by the following:

> ... an entire society decides which vocations deserve true professional status. If that is true, it is impossible for proponents, opponents or scholars sitting on the sidelines to make this decision until or unless society as a whole is ready to make it. Of the characteristics examined (in the article), only two appear fairly consistently to have governed society's decisions and at the same time to have furnished society with the requisites of a profession.[39]

This author goes on to suggest the two requisites used by society; namely, the practitioners must be paid directly for the services or commodities they sell, and society must have direct control over the right to practice. In speaking of barriers to profession status faced by the insurance industry, another writer applied somewhat different tests (public service, educational requirements, and codes of ethics), but he expressed a very common feeling about the importance of public recognition:

> We cannot say we are professionals because this is, in the end, a status that is conferred by the public on a particular group. If the public does not recognize us as a profession, nothing we can say will gain that coveted status for our group.[40]

39. William Peet, *CPCU Annals,* Fall 1960, op. cit., pp. 171-72.
40. Ronald T. Anderson, "The Professional Urge," *CPCU Annals,* Vol. 29, No. 6, June 1976, p. 121.

The reader will note, in both of these quotations, the idea that profession status cannot be self-declared by the group itself, or even by outsiders, if the general public disagrees. Of course, it is entirely possible to have profession status within a group; it just would not be worth much without wider recognition.

The seeking of instant recognition has led some rather disreputable occupations to rely entirely on advertising and public relations campaigns, as though a billion dollar advertising budget could buy profession status for any group, whereas the majority of aspirants with a fighting chance for public recognition seem to accept as fact that it must first be earned. As to the best way for a group to "earn" the distinction, there is considerably less agreement. Again, one major reason for this disagreement is the fuzziness with which the "public" is defined, as well as the lack of hard evidence on which standards the public uses.

From this writer's perspective, the public's role in determining a profession would be a fertile area for in-depth research. To say that the profession status of an occupation is conferred by public recognition is to say very little. Indeed, one yearns to know whether the advantages of group recognition are worth the costs. One would first need to know, specifically, the exact "public" which decides the question of recognition. One would then need to know the standards this public uses in making the decision, as well as the relative weight or importance of each standard in this public's eye. In the absence of such data, your author is unwilling to entrust the *idea* of a profession to any public opinion poll. Some of the finest books in history never made anybody's best seller list, and some which did would not be able to pass any other meaningful test of good literature. Musicians have stayed at the top of the record charts for years, as popular entertainers, with music "talents" which would be judged as poor or mediocre by highly skilled and highly disciplined musicians (and this should not all be dismissed as mere jealousy). Racism is very prevalent among all races, but this does not make it right and proper, or even a characteristic to be desired. Similarly, if profession status is to be decided by the number of people who "buy" it, like a best seller list, occupations seeking the status may find that the advantages are outweighed by the compromises it may require.

For example, careful research might reveal that the public accepts occupations as professions based primarily on their television image, the life and death drama of their work, the fact that they must meet rigorous occupational licensure requirements just to "practice," their high incomes, their political power, the large public demand for their services, whether the work seems to be interesting and challenging, the fact that they do not knock on your door to solicit business, the fact that they charge fees, or other characteristics perceived by the public. Are *all* of these characteristics desirable to the aspirants of profession status?

Table 1-1

Honesty and Ethical Standards of Eleven Occupations*

Percent of total nationwide sample who rated occupations as very high or high; average; low or very low in honesty and ethical standards.

	Very High or High	Average	Low or Very Low
Medical doctors	56%	35%	9%
Engineers	49	43	4
College teachers	44	44	9
Journalists	33	49	16
Lawyers	25	48	26
Building contractors	23	54	21
Business executives	20	58	20
Senators	19	51	29
Congressmen	14	47	38
Labor union leaders	12	38	48
Advertising practitioners	11	43	44

*Adapted from "The Gallup Opinion Index," Political, Social and Economic Trends, Report No. 134, September 1976, pp. 17-29. Perhaps out of charity, Dr. Gallup did not include the clergy in his listing. Unfortunately, for our purposes, there were no separate ratings for the insurance industry or for particular occupational categories within the industry.

Are they the only desirable traits? What if the public left out or gave very small weight to education? What if they gave comparatively little weight to ethics? If that sounds far-fetched, consider the excerpt from a recent Gallup opinion poll, where people were asked to rate the "honesty and ethical standards" of individuals in eleven occupations, in Table 1-1.

While the "no opinion" column is not shown above, it is significant that very few people said they had no opinion (less than 2 percent each for most of the occupations listed). Of particular interest are the ratings for medical doctors and lawyers, the two most widely recognized as professions of the eleven occupations. Doctors were at the very top of the list; yet only a slight majority of the people gave the honesty and ethical standards of doctors high or very high ratings. Lawyers were given a slightly higher percentage of low or very low ratings than they were high or very high ratings, and the highest ratings of lawyers were less than half the comparable ratings for doctors. Both groups got a surprisingly high percentage of average ratings.[41]

The Gallup survey results become even more intersting when we compare them with the prestige ratings of the 1978 Harris poll, cited earlier. Harris found that 90 percent of the people regard doctors as having "very great or considerable *prestige*." Gallup results say only 56 percent felt doctors have "very high or high" *honesty and ethical standards*. Some 73 percent feel lawyers get the highest prestige ratings, whereas only 25 percent feel they deserve the highest honesty and ethics ratings. Of course, there are some dangers in comparing the sample results of two different organizations, and there are doubtless some sampling errors in each of the surveys. But suppose they had asked a statistically representative sample of the entire population the following question: "Which of the following occupations are *true professions?*" One suspects that nearly 100 percent of the people might have said medical doctors and lawyers are true professions. If so, in the light of the other evidence summarized above, it appears that people may not place much weight on honesty and ethical standards when they are deciding which occupations they accept as professions or prestigious. It would not necessarily mean that people have a low regard for honesty and ethics. It would seem to mean that they put as much or more weight on other factors which they perceive as characteristics of true professions. Or, it could mean that traditional professions are still regarded as such, but losing their social status. Or, it could mean some vastly different things which are not readily apparent in the data now available. What is apparent is the need for new and reliable research data.

In the meantime, it would seem only prudent to focus on the *desirable* characteristics of the profession idea. Apart from what the public thinks about the totality of a given occupation at any time, these desirable characteristics need to be sharpened, so that they may better serve as worthwhile goals for individuals and occupational associations.

CHARACTERISTICS OF A PROFESSION: A BRIEF SUMMARY

Since the foregoing discussion of profession characteristics has been lengthy, a brief summary may be in order. The occupational idea of a profession is probably best defined by identifying its set of distinguishing characteristics. The idea of a profession emerges more clearly when

---

41. Not shown above are various other tables in the Gallup survey results, which reveal important variations in the honesty and ethics ratings according to the income, age, educational level, politics, geographical location, occupation, race, and sex of the persons doing the rating.

these characteristics are viewed together as a collective set, because some of the characteristics are not unique to professions. The characteristics identified here were as follows:

1. A commitment to high ethical standards;
2. A prevailing attitude of altruism;
3. Mandatory educational preparation and training;
4. Mandatory continuing education;
5. A formal association or society;
6. Independence; and, with reservations,
7. Public recognition as a profession.

There is some overlap among these characteristics, and no attempt was made to make them mutually exclusive and collectively exhaustive categories of formal logic. Each was considered by the author to be worthy of separate treatment. Other authors use somewhat different lists.

Above all, these are *desirable* characteristics of a profession. They are not absolute prerequisites, because (a) no established profession meets all the criteria perfectly, (b) some unrecognized occupations meet some or all of the criteria fairly well and (c) there are considerable differences in the degrees to which each criterion is met among the established professions. Each characteristic also poses a number of questions which have not yet been answered satisfactorily.

No conscious attempt has been made to assign relative weights or priorities to each and every characteristic. However, the general notions of competence and ethics standards are almost universally agreed to be at the top of the importance scale. Mandatory *continuing* education is the newest of the characteristics to be identified, yet it may soon be widely recognized as one of the most important attributes by which to judge whether an occupation deserves the title of profession. The oldest item on the list, public recognition, undoubtedly started the search to find what it is that is distinctive about theology, law, and medicine. Whether public recognition is thought of as a prerequisite to social status, the goal to be achieved by an occupation having specified characteristics or just one of several characteristics which are desirable, the notion of "public" recognition has not been defined well enough to determine the nature and extent of its role. Allowing a public majority to define the idea of a profession is a particularly debatable approach if one's reason for defining profession is to find desirable characteristics to aspire to and emulate. More reliable research data would be very helpful, if not essential, in the resolution of the remaining, troublesome and largely unanswered questions concerning the profession-public recognition relationship.

INSURANCE AND
THE CHARACTERISTICS OF A PROFESSION

A few members of recognized professions have shared in published works their concerns about a potential loss of profession status.[42] Vastly larger numbers of pages have been occupied by commentaries on the aspirants to profession status. In this respect, the insurance industry need not feel lonely. A long list of occupations marks the ceaseless indulgence in the exercise of putting them to various tests of profession adequacy.[43]

For three reasons, this section will be brief. First, there is a very ample supply of published commentary on the extent to which the insurance industry has, or does not have, the desirable characteristics of a profession.[44] Second, to put the tape measure on the insurance industry as a whole does not take much time. One does not need to go much further than the notion of *mandatory* educational preparation and training as a precondition of the right to "practice insurance." A significant segment of the industry clearly does not measure up to this or other accepted characteristics of a profession. Moreover, those who still want proof would not be convinced by anything which has not already been said. Third, a rehash of what others have expressed better would blow this ship off course.

One constantly struggles at the wheel to keep the trip interesting without losing sight of the pilot's destination. But the reader, as well,

---

42. One thoughtful example is provided by W.A. Paton, "Earmarks of a Profession — And the APB," *The Journal of Accountancy,* January 1971, pp. 37-45. Paton is concerned about activities of the Accounting Principles Board which may impair the professional status of public accountants and the quality of services rendered by CPAs. Specifically, he worries about the erosion of professional independence among public accountants.

43. For examples in a field closely related to insurance, see Douglas A. Hayes, "Potential for Profession Status"; Marshall D. Ketchum, "Is Financial Analysis A Profession?"; and C. Steward Sheppard, "The Professionalization of the Financial Analyst," all in the November-December 1967 issue of the *Financial Analysts Journal.*

44. For a cross-section of opinions, see Ronald T. Anderson, "The "Professional Urge," op. cit.; William Peet, "Insurance—Present or Potential Profession," op. cit.; Patricia P. Douglas, "Professionalism: Its Presence and Absence in the Insurance Industry," op. cit.; and Edwin S. Overman, "The Professional Concept and Business Ethics," op. cit. See also William E. Brandow, "Insurance as a Profession," *CPCU Annals,* Vol. 17, No. 4, Winter 1964, pp. 374-75; and Duke N. Stern and David R. Klock, "Public Policy and the Professionalization of Life Underwriters," *American Business Law Journal,* Vol. 13, 1975, pp. 225-38.

has the right to know where we are headed. So, perhaps it would be wise to describe the next port.

It soon will become obvious that the next chapter is rigged. It will make no apologies for trying to make you and me think deep thoughts about ourselves, as *individuals*. Elbert Hubbard once said: "If I supply you with a thought, you may remember it and you may not. But if I can make you think a thought for yourself, I have indeed added to your stature." In the chapter the reader is about to complete, much was said about the idea of a profession as an occupational group. A few thoughts were supplied. Many questions were raised to stimulate additional thinking. However, if the effort was successful, it served to pave the way for the more personal and important notion of professionalism, each individual's quest for an unrealized and worthwhile ideal. As Aldous Huxley said, "There's only one corner of the universe you can be certain of improving, and that's your own self." It would be arrogant and presumptuous, indeed, for this author to suggest a bundle of neat little rules for improving one's self, even in connection with the smaller tasks of one's occupational pursuits. What one can hope to do is serve up a small but solid chunk of meat to chew on.

CHAPTER 2

Professionalism
and the Professional

The heights by great men reached and kept
Were not attained by sudden flight,
But they, while their companions slept,
Were toiling upward in the night.
—Longfellow

The preceding chapter stressed the idea of a profession as a distinctive occupational *group*. Although such a group may be identified by a set of desirable characteristics, individuals within the group may or may not qualify for profession status. Truly, significant differences in the degrees of professional competence and ethics can be found among the individual members of every profession. There are likewise varying degrees of competence and ethics among individual members of occupations which are not widely recognized as professions. And virtually every occupation has its share of incompetent charlatans and highly competent thieves. These are facts of life. Consequently, there is little to be gained by the common and indefensible pretense that the desirable characteristics of an occupational group belong to everyone who pays the annual membership fee. Such characteristics, in the end, have their greatest value as definers of standards which each *individual* may seek to achieve, if he or she desires them and is willing to pay the price.

PROFESSIONALISM

As a part of speech, "professionalism" is a noun. It is a word used to denote the conduct, aims, or qualities which mark or characterize a professional. A "professional," in turn, is a person who conforms to the technical and ethical standards of a profession. Professional*ism* refers to the qualities themselves; a professio*nal* is a person who has the specified qualities.

It was suggested earlier that a profession is an occupational group which has, in varying degrees, the following desirable characteristics: a commitment to high ethical standards; a prevailing attitude of altruism; mandatory educational preparation and training; mandatory continuing education; a formal association or society; independence; and, (subject to the author's reservations) public recognition as a profession. For the purpose of translating these into a workable notion of professionalism, it is both necessary and helpful to shorten and simplify the list of applicable characteristics. One needs to dispense with the group orientation and concentrate, instead, on the qualities which characterize the professional as an individual with a personal identity, an identity which is separate and distinct from the group(s) of which the individual may be a part.

The many advantages of a formal association or society have already been acknowledged. The belonger who actively participates in the functions of a formal association will reap many personal rewards, not the least of which is the opportunity to serve others who are inside and outside the group. But trade associations per se, valuable as they may be for other purposes, do not get to the core of the idea of professionalism, and professional societies suffer from two important handicaps. First, though such societies frequently have high admissions standards, most of them do not regulate the right to practice an occupation, and they do not control certification (i.e., the conferring of specialty and professional designations). It follows that their power to enforce professional standards is limited to the power of expulsion of individuals from membership in the society. Moreover, the expulsion of members can hurt the society more than the individuals who are expelled, by reducing the number of dues-paying members without affecting the former members' right to practice the occupation.

Second, *membership* in a professional society is not as essential to the idea of professional*ism* as it is to the group idea of a profession. One can certainly argue that a professional has an *ethical* obligation to assist in maintaining and raising the professional standards of his or her occupation, but this notion does not need to be a separate characteristic of professionalism, since it is easily folded into the ethics characteristic. A more troublesome issue is whether any ethics code should require professionals to be members of specified professional societies. Although it would be impossible for most professional societies to impose such a requirement on nonmembers, many society leaders have been tempted by the possibilities of getting membership in their own society imposed as an ethical or legal requirement of state licensing boards, national specialty certification boards, organizations conferring professional designations, and/or educational institutions. The reluctance of the latter organizations to oblige the societies is perfectly understandable. Society *membership* per se seldom has any appreciable influence on the professional's competence and ethics, and requiring the professional to belong to a particular society is felt to be a serious infringement on his or her professional independence. It also would be difficult to require membership in one society, because each occupation normally has several societies for which the professional is eligible. Should a physician, for instance, be required to join the American Medical Association? Other medical societies? Many physicians have been harshly critical of the AMA's involvement in various political matters. A physician could even feel ethically obligated *not* to belong to the AMA. In any case, it is abundantly clear that a physician can be highly competent and ethical without belonging to the AMA, which brings us back to the central point, to wit: membership in a particular society is not essential to the *idea* of professionalism. To the extent that society membership requirements are considered essential by a given occupation, they should be treated as part of a broader ethics characteristic, not as a separate quality of professionalism. The assertion that they "should" be so treated is deliberate here, if only to force a brief consideration of the alternatives.

One extreme is represented by the dictionary definition of professionalism, which is far too general either to apply in our daily lives or to define the idea. The other extreme would be a lengthy list of specific qualities for each and every occupation. Such a list invariably takes the form of an ethics code that sets the standards to which the individual is expected to conform. While this writer would be the last to deny the important role of ethics codes, and while much of the remainder of this essay is devoted to them, it is the commitment to observe such codes which all aspirants to professionalism have in common, not the specific code standards themselves. In fact, the codes of various occupations probably should be different, so that they will best address any unique needs of each occupation. But that is exactly what makes the *specifics* of each code too different to incorporate in a common notion of professionalism. Some occupations may wish to require society membership. Others may think such a requirement would be unethical or otherwise unprofessional. Thus, in the interest of defining professionalism as an idea which may be applied by individuals in every occupation, one "should" concentrate on the desirable qualities that are common to all occupations.

When the public recognition characteristic of a profession is considered in the context of an individual, two aspects of public recognition come to mind. The first is not a quality of the professionalism idea. The second is just a part of a more fundamental quality.

The first aspect has to do with the well-known and significant fact that many people are motivated to seek the qualities of professionalism largely because they want to be publicly recognized as professionals. For some individuals, such public recognition may even be the only motivation toward professionalism. In either case, it is not a quality *of* professionalism. It is a goal or reason for seeking it. The second aspect of public recognition concerns the tangible recognition which comes from *earning* degrees and designations such as M.D., CPCU, CLU, or CPA. This is a most significant aspect of public recognition, to be sure, but it is not really a separate quality of professionalism. It is better thought of as a "proof-positive" part of the professional competence and ethics qualities of professionalism. That is to say, such degrees and designations give tangible evidence to laymen that their holders have met the qualifying standards which each degree of designation entails. *To that extent,* they have earned a measure of professional status.

Mandatory continuing education, as well as mandatory formal preparation and training, can be thought of as aspects of the more fundamental notion of professional competence. This simplification is not only logical. It also has the advantage of permitting a broader perspective on the various types, degrees, and sources of professional competence among various occupations. Different occupations may require, of aspirants to professional status within the occupations, different mixes of manual and mental skills, different types of preparation and training and varying degrees of preparation, apprenticeship, and subsequent work experience. Yet, in every occupation, professional competence is central to the idea of professionalism. It is a quality to be acquired and maintained by every deserving professional.

Altruism, an unselfish concern for the welfare of others, is frequently treated as a separate quality of professionalism. Some writers also treat "performance" as a separate quality, on the admittedly logical grounds that a true professional is not merely a competent spectator sitting on the sidelines. The real professional is a performer, and he or she lives up to high standards of performance. However, in order to define professionalism broadly enough to be equally applicable to all occupations, it is helpful to view altruism and performance, along with the concept of independence, as elements of the more fundamental quality of professional ethics. Altruism is more of a theme or broad goal of ethics codes, whereas performance and independence are standards which are necessary to achieve broad and specific goals of a professional nature. Again, the specific ethics standards are better left to each occupation, because professionalism in different occupations may require different standards of altruism, performance, and professional independence.

PRIMARY CHARACTERISTICS
OF THE PROFESSIONAL

When the focus of attention is on the desirable qualities which may be possessed by individuals in virtually every occupation, it becomes apparent that professional competence and ethics are fundamental qualities of professionalism. Implicitly, this formulation invites the hasty conclusion that a "professional" is a person who meets the *minimum* competence and ethics standards which are required to obtain and maintain the right to practice the occupation in question. But acceptance of such a conclusion would lead full circle back to the common usage of a dictionary definition, and it would mean that a "professional" is any person who is employed for compensation. A person who lost the right to practice one occupation could still be a "professional," simply by getting another job with lesser competence and ethics requirements. The customary way to avoid this conclusion is to assert that such an individual is not a "true" professional. The trouble is, the very same convenience of language is used, in a sharply contradictory way, in referring to practicing lawyers and physicians as the only "true" professionals, despite the fact that some among them do not even meet the minimum standards of their own professions (they just have not been caught, yet).

The paradox here is rather easily explained. Many of those who use the term "true" professional are trying, often self-servingly, to reserve professional status exclusively for *all* members of a limited number of occupations. In contrast, your author wishes to reserve the term "professional" for a limited number of individuals in a large number of occupations. There is little to be achieved by the preoccupation with learned vocations, while there is a lot to be gained by emphasizing the deserving individual in every honorable vocation. Who, then, is the "deserving" individual? What are the "honorable" vocations?

Since observance of the bare minimum standards of competence and ethics would not make any individual special, extraordinary, or admirable, let us first stipulate that *honorable and high standards of professional competence and ethics are the most essential qualities of professionalism.* Accordingly, the deserving professional is a person who meets and maintains competence and ethics standards which are significantly higher than the minimums required to engage in the occupation, and the standards themselves are honorable, i.e., capable of honor. When it is presumed or understood that the author is implicitly thinking of honorable standards, the primary characteristics of a deserving professional may be reduced to two, as follows: *A professional is an individual who (1) has a high level of competence and (2) adheres to high ethical standards in the application of that competence.* Above all else, these two qualities distinguish the deserving professional from the ordinary merchant of products or services. Once a professional, always a professional? Not necessarily! An individual "has" professional competence at a point in time. Unless it is maintained and improved, it may be lost more easily than it was acquired. Moreover, the quality of competence is inexorably interrelated to the quality of ethics, if only because competence is an ethical obligation which is owed to those whom it is the professional's duty or privilege to serve in a professional capacity. Stated another way, individuals who hold themselves out to the public as "professionals" have an ethical duty of competence; otherwise, they are engaging in a factual misrepresentation of the worst sort.

One of the essential qualities of professionalism cannot be held by individuals who work in occupations which a democratic society has declared illegal. The murderer for hire, the seller of harmful drugs to children, and the petty thief may be highly competent in their fields. They may even be admired in some quarters. But neither their occupations nor their ethical standards are ultimately capable of honor. However, this author categorically rejects the snobbish and condescending view that professionalism is the exclusive property of individuals who are engaged in the traditional professions or other learned occupations. Both of the essential qualities of professionalism may be held by the construction worker, the surgeon, the secretary, the judge, the used car dealer, the minister, the insurance agent, the engineer, the senator, the journalist, the supermarket manager, and the clerk alike. To deny the aspiration of professionalism to the used car dealer is to miss the point. No truly learned person would attempt such a denial, for it would deny the car dealer the human satisfaction of an altruistic concern for his customers and the opportunity to pay his daughter's way to medical school. Furthermore, every truly learned person realizes that the moral measure of a man or woman goes far beyond the occupation in which each is engaged, despite the fact that his or her morality may be reflected in its pursuit. If dairy farming is a "lesser" calling than obstetrics, then obstetrics is a lesser calling than motherhood. If the lawyer who defends the twice-convicted rapist is engaged in a "higher" calling, the lawyer is less to be admired than the competent and ethical television repairman who can also be trusted alone with the lawyer's wife. No, a person's worth or morality is not measured by the number of years he spends in school or the number of degrees he holds. Nor should the notion of professionalism be confined to those whose calling it is to engage in a learned vocation. Indeed, learning alone is not the measure of professional competence. Persons in some fields may be highly competent without much formal learning. *No* person may be competent without the skills which his or her occupation requires. And every competent person who deserves the label "professional" is deeply committed to high standards of professional ethics.

THE PRICE OF PROFESSIONALISM

Generally

Professionalism does not come to its seekers free of "charge." It exacts standards for which all aspirants will have to pay the toll. Furthermore, the price of professionalism will not be the same for every occupation. The larger prices will be paid by members of occupations which (1) require extensive learning and/or (2) involve more complex questions of ethics. Yet, the nonmonetary benefits to the professional may ultimately be the same in every honorable occupation.

Surgeons who wish to specialize in organ transplants must first spend many years in school, meet internship and hospital residency requirements, work long hours, develop extraordinary manual skills, and make many personal sacrifices along the way. Their incomes will be larger than most, but they also face some of the most complex ethical choices. Appreciably smaller learning and skill demands, as well as simpler ethical choices, may lower the price of professionalism for the kindergarten teacher, the photo engraver, the typist, or the concrete finisher of a construction crew. Nonetheless, the deserving professional in all these fields, beyond the price each pays, can reap the priceless benefits of blending extraordinary competence with extraordinary ethical standards. Each will know the pride and satisfaction of a durable job well done in the service of others. Call it the personal rewards of altruism, if you wish, or the necessity of "man's humanity to man." Or, perhaps there is an even better and more direct explanation. In the pursuit of an occupation, an individual can truly care for others only by combining the competence and ethics ingredients of professionalism. And men and women must care for others, if they are ultimately to care for themselves.

For Insurance Professionals

Insurance professionals are in an enviable position in many respects. They may know all of the ultimate rewards of caring for others. They normally pay a smaller price than the surgeon does for professionalism, yet they may make a substantial amount of money, some more than the surgeon. Insurance professionals also have the satisfaction of knowing that they serve vital needs of mankind. It would be stretching a point to contend that every insurance professional directly serves a more vital need than the physician, the clergyman, or the defense attorney. However, one could certainly argue that the insurance advisor serves more vital and more universal needs than the lawyer or the accountant does in the rendering of advice to others. While insurance alone cannot save a life, it can pay for the medical treatment that will. Insurance can hold families together. It can permit the mother to raise the children of their deceased father without being forced to take a job. It can replace the income of a disabled breadwinner, send a son or daughter to medical or law school, pay for quality medical and legal care. It can protect the owners of homes and automobiles from lawsuits. It can replace the dwelling destroyed by windstorm so that the family will have a decent place to live. It can, indeed, protect the individual, the family, the business, the law firm, the medical firm, the accounting firm, and the church from financial ruin. But such things cannot be achieved by the insurance advisor alone. The quantity and quality of insurance necessarily and heavily depends upon underwriters, claims representatives, safety engineers, company executives, and many other insurance professionals. Additionally, proper insurance protection depends upon the proper education and training of insurance professionals *and* insurance consumers.

The need of insurance practitioners for education and training, along with the public's need for proof thereof, has had an obvious effect on the way insurance professionalism has been defined. A growing number of people obviously feel that insurance professionalism is the meeting of the standards initially required to obtain the CPCU, CLU, FSA, FCAS, or similar professional designations. Thus, they tend to view the price of insurance professionalism as the price of obtaining such designations.

There can be little doubt that obtaining an *earned* professional designation involves the sort of "blood, sweat, and tears" which men and women will not engage in without strong motivations. Those who fear failure may not even try, and those who fail examinations may give up in despair. The designations demand personal sacrifices, monetary costs, and long hours of quiet study. The latter poses a dilemma of particular import to the family man or woman. Single individuals need only resolve that professional studies are more important to them than the alternative ways they would otherwise spend their leisure time. Married persons, especially those with small children, have family obligations to consider. The natural tendency is to rationalize that professional studies will ultimately benefit the family more than would the spending of the same amount of time in ministering to the needs of the spouse and children. Dr. Noah Langdale, President of Georgia State University, put the matter into perspective with the following cogent observation: "There is no success outside one's family that will compensate for a failure with it." Since a failure with one's family is too high a price to pay for professionalism, perhaps one way to resolve the dilemma is suggested by the Longfellow quotation at the beginning of this chapter. It is the notion that great men and women reach and maintain great heights only by "toiling upward in the night." Such toiling, in the late of night or the first breath of morning, does not require one to ignore his or her family. Toil is a price of professionalism, however, and it requires a willingness to sacrifice at least some of the time one would otherwise spend at the bowling alley, at the golf course, or in front of a television set.

There are other potential consequences of insurance professionalism which have not been widely discussed in insurance circles, at least not as "prices" of professionalism. Four such prices will be briefly described under the following headings: the increasing vulnerability to the unauthorized practice of law; the increasing vulnerability to professional liability in tort; the growing demands for proof of continuing professional competence; and, the price of adherence to increasingly demanding codes of professional ethics. The first of these prices or costs of professionalism probably has greater impact on life insurance producers. The second has impact on all insurance producers and company executives. The third and fourth are prices which are likely to be paid by all insurance practitioners who desire to achieve and maintain the essential qualities of professionalism.

Concerning the unauthorized practice of law, Dr. Snider aptly observes: " ... the life underwriter may be tempted to serve his client in those areas beyond the limit of his authority but well within the scope of his knowledge and training."[45] A life underwriter who has completed CLU and post-CLU courses will have studied, in addition to individual and group life and health insurance, pension planning, wills, trusts, estates, taxation, economics, investments, and life insurance law; and, equally important, he or she will have demonstrated an ability to *apply* these areas to the financial needs of clients. The life insurance professional who does the best job for clients is the most likely to be accused of the unauthorized practice of law. Yet, other than prohibitions against the acceptance of insurance commissions, practicing attorneys may (and do) give all sorts of life insurance and retirement planning advice, despite the fact that the vast majority of law schools do not require education or training in either area. The "team approach" to estate planning seems to be gaining ground among responsible life insurance agents, attorneys, trust officers, CPAs and investment advisors, but its merits are by no means as widely accepted among the traditional profes-

---

45. H. Wayne Snider, "Problems of Professionalism," *The Journal of Insurance,* Vol. XXX, No. 4, December 1963, p. 566. For an excellent analysis of how a life underwriter may avoid or engage in the unauthorized practice of law, see Ralph J. Chittick, "Responsibilities of Professionalism," *The Journal of the American Society of C.L.U.,* Winter 1964, esp. pp. 35-40.

sions as they are among CLUs. In the meantime, life insurance agents will continue to face the dilemma of better serving clients at the risk of the unauthorized practice of law.

All insurance producers are also exposed, increasingly, to the legal consequences of their negligence. Under the law of torts, professionals have long been held to higher standards of care than nonprofessionals.[46] Therein lies another potential price of professionalism. To the extent that insurance practitioners succeed in convincing the public that they are professionals, they may become increasingly vulnerable in professional negligence suits.[47] Such vulnerability has already affected not only insurance producers but also the corporate officers and directors of insurance companies.

Every insurance practitioner must face the growing pressures for proof of *continuing* competence long after the obtaining of CPCU or CLU designations. Because the development of mandatory continuing education was discussed at length in the previous chapter, it will not be repeated here. Suffice it to say that the American Institute's new Code of Professional Ethics imposes upon CPCUs an ethical obligation to maintain their professional competence. It stops short of requiring them to certify such competence periodically, as has already been done by other professions. It does not require or provide for voluntary self-assessment examinations. Nor does it require or provide for peer review. However, all of these means of proving continuing competence are rapidly being adopted by many professions, through an ethics code or otherwise. And any or all of these means may also become part of the price of insurance professionalism, sooner or later, voluntarily or by statute. As Palmer observed:

> ... it should be clear that *the public no longer takes any of the professions for granted. The public is demanding proof of concern for*

---

46. The liability exposures of professionals are discussed in CPCU 4, which also deals with the liability exposures of corporate officers and directors. See Donald Malecki, James Donaldson and Ronald Horn, *Commercial Liability Risk Management and Insurance,* American Institute for Property and Liability Underwriters, Inc., 1978.
47. For a recent case in point, see *Tannenbaum v. Provident Mutual Life Insurance Co.,* 53 App. Div. 2d 86, 386 N.Y.S. 2d 409 (1976), aff'd mem, No. 218 (May 5, 1977). In its ruling, the court noted that the insured had relied heavily on the agent, and the court also stressed that as a CLU, the agent had a special duty of care and disclosure to the applicant. The potential implications for CPCUs should be obvious! For an analysis of earlier court decisions, see Ralph J. Chittick, "Responsibilities of Professionalism," op. cit., pp. 29-35.

their interest. That concern must be evidenced by results, not conversation.[48] (emphasis supplied)

That the public no longer takes any of the professions for granted is an unmistakable trend, if not a current fact of life. Members of the public are beginning to make distinctions. They are beginning to focus more on the demonstrable ethics and competence of each professional, as an individual, and they seem to want tangible proof of concern for the public interest. All this is happening at the very same time when insurance practitioners are doing their utmost to convince everyone that they are professionals. The implications should be rather obvious. Insurance professionalism is likely to demand much more rigorous forms of public accountability than have been historically supposed.

Finally, there are the potential costs of adherence to increasingly demanding codes of professional ethics. Written codes of ethics have existed for many years. Some of them have never been enforced. Some, indeed, offer little more than a superficial and insincere lip service to broad and vague standards which attempt to anoint the members of an organization with the indisputable virtues of motherhood, country, morality, and the good dog, Lassie. Among codes which have been enforced or otherwise adhered to, some have had to be revised due to the results or threats of antitrust actions. Trade association codes have historically provided numerous illustrations of conspiracies in restraint of trade and other antisocial restrictions of competition. More recently, the traditional professions have been taken to task for such things as uniform minimum fee schedules, ethics code prohibitions of advertising, and other practices with similar effects. A great many trades have adopted new codes of ethics, while traditional and newer professions have effected massive overhauls of their previously existing codes. In fact, ethics code adoptions and revisions seem to have totally dominated the activities of literally hundreds of occupational organizations during the early 1970s. They have been busy at the task of defining and altering the standards themselves. They have been changing their disciplinary rules and procedures to comply with the constitutional requirements of due process, and some have been attempting to toughen enforcement practices, procedures, and penalties.

With the notable exception of the codes of membership organizations which do not have strong enforcement powers (e.g., the American Medical Association), professional ethics codes generally seem to be moving in the direction of making greater demands on the individuals to whom they apply. Especially in the most recent revisions of the ethics code of

---

48. Russell E. Palmer, "It's Time to Stop Talking," *The Journal of Accountancy,* October 1975, p. 65.

CPAs, one finds considerably less self-protectionism and a much greater emphasis on the welfare of the public at large. One also finds evidence, among the recognized professions, of a growing resolve to put teeth in the ethics enforcement mechanisms. Such developments have not exactly been celebrated by all whom they directly affect. They have been met by angry and irrational cries of protest. And, at the other extreme, they have provoked thoughtful concerns about whether the additional restrictions on professional independence are really in the public interest. The latter concerns may force a healthy recognition of the need of professions to redefine their traditional notions of professional independence. Further restrictions of professional independence, along with adherence to higher standards of ethics generally, are likely to emerge as modern prices of professionalism.

Many people have drawn hasty and superficial conclusions about the question of why there has been such a marked increase in the public's interest in occupational ethics. For instance, hundreds of journalists and media personalities, through their endless utterings, turned the phrase "Watergate morality" into a popular cliché. They likewise showed a fondness for the indefensible contention that this sort of "morality" is unique in our society, particularly among presidents and high public officials. Then, with additional revelations which confirmed that wrongdoings had become more of an epidemic than a unique disease, the phrases "Watergate morality" and the "new morality" became catchalls to describe widespread corruption among Washington lawyers and politicians.[49]

The thoughtful columnist, Vermont Royster, was one of the few who was able to penetrate the two-edged wall of political bias which surrounded the underlying issues. Other journalists had already acknowledged the widespread existence of the phenomenon in virtually every occupation.[50] Few had dealt so openly with the nature of the phenome-

---

49. Years before Watergate appeared in the national spotlight, scholars had already exploded the myth that there is anything new about the "new morality" (which makes one wonder whether some very prominent newspaper journalists ever read anything beyond the newspapers). To take just one for instance that falls into the category of "must" reading for insurance professionals, see John D. Long, "Insurance and the New Morality," *CPCU Annals,* December 1970, pp. 303-21. Dr. Long, a CPCU for whom this writer has great affection and respect, suggests that a resurgence of the new morality poses a long-range threat to the proper functioning of the insurance mechanism. Though Dr. Long has authored numerous other publications on the insurance-ethics relationship, the cited article has particular relevance to the nature of widespread ethical relativism in our society.

non. Though it is a lengthy quotation extracted from a longer article, it truly deserves the reader's careful evaluation:

> ... the shock, I believe, was not so much that a few lawyers might deliberately violate the law; there are shysters in every profession and craft. Rather it was that so many of them seemed to go astray unthinkingly. Their behavior was not that of the intentionally dishonest man, the bank robber who knows full well what he is doing. Rather it arose from *a kind of moral myopia that led them to do things without seeing any ethical questions at all....*
>
> It's true, of course, there's nothing novel in immoral behavior.... Corruption is as old as civilization. *The difference lies in the morality we profess. Today for so many people in so many places corruption steals upon them unawares. They are not so much consciously immoral as unconsciously amoral.*
>
> *If there's any moral standard at all today it lies in the doctrine that short of obvious injury to another one is free to do one's thing.* That has an appealing sound, but under such a standard how does one teach the young not to cheat?
>
> Under this morality ... no moral injunction comes with any authority ... *whatever one does to one's self, is free from moral fault.*
>
> This also absolves guilt for the corruption of others. The dope pusher excuses himself by saying if I don't push it someone else will. Not far different from saying if I don't pay this bribe somebody else will. *Besides, if everybody's doing it, who is to be blamed?*
>
> We have come to this by a devious route. We began in good cause to remove the law's punishment for people's private conduct. But *having removed the law's proscription we have come to say what is not proscribed is to be approved, even promoted.* We began by asking sympathy for the misguided thief or murderer, we end by excusing theft or murder by the misguided....
>
> The danger here is that every society, from the most primitive to the most advanced, depends for its survival on an accepted moral base.... Without a sense that some things are wrong simply because they are wrong ... I am tempted to say, without a sense of sin — then every man is cast adrift. Not just the young; the lawyer, doctor or public servant has no inner standard to measure whether what he does is ethical or unethical. Why should we be surprised, then, at what some men do?

---

50. For example, on the front page of *The Wall Street Journal,* June 10, 1975, there is a prominent reference to a study conducted by Archie Carroll, a professor at the University of Georgia. Professor Carroll reportedly found that three out of five of the corporate executives surveyed said that young managers would have committed the same kind of unethical acts that the junior Nixon aides committed. A striking 65 percent of the executives agreed that managers today feel under pressure to compromise personal standards to achieve company goals.

> I do not know why we have gone so far on this road. . . . But to look around at the common behavior is to see what we have put in jeopardy.[51] (all emphasis is supplied)

Yes, it is tempting to conclude that the rampant corruption of Washington lawyers and politicians provided a rude public awakening to the ultimate dangers of "doing one's own thing." But if it did, it was only because many people saw the same kind of corruption in their neighbors, in their families, and in themselves. Perhaps there is, at last, a growing sense of a critical need to make vast changes in the ethical standards which individuals and occupations "profess." If not, perhaps the renewed interest in written codes of ethics is at least one giant step in the right direction.

A SUMMARY

Professionalism is a concept which refers to the qualities which mark or characterize a professional. Despite the historical tendency to reserve professionalism for all members of the recognized learned professions, your author has argued that honorable and high standards of professional competence and ethics are the most essential qualities of professionalism. Accordingly, a professional is an individual who (1) has a high level of professional competence and (2) adheres to high ethical standards in the application of that competence.

The personal benefits of professionalism go far beyond the increased financial returns it may bring to its achievers. The larger benefits come from a personal pride in excellent craftsmanship, the deep inner satisfactions of serving the needs of others, and the knowledge that individuals will care for themselves only if they care for others.

While the nonmonetary benefits of professionalism are ultimately the same for members of every honorable occupation, the price paid for professionalism is likely to be larger for members of occupations which involve extensive learning and complicated questions of ethics. For

---

51. Vermont Royster, "The Common Behavior," *The Wall Street Journal,* September 17, 1975. See also Floyd G. Lawrence, "Whose Ethics Guide Business,"*Industry Week,* October 27, 1975, wherein an extensive survey shows that an overwhelming majority of business managers feel that "they are a better judge than anyone else of what's right and wrong for them." Theoretical writers were concluding, at about the same time, that executive behavior is "learned in significant degree through observation." See George Strother, "The Moral Codes of Executives: A Watergate-inspired Look at Barnard's Theory of Executive Responsibility," the *Academy of Management Review,* Vol. 1, No. 2, April 1976 (submitted on June 20, 1975).

insurance practitioners, the prices or costs of professionalism may include the following:

1. the necessity of extensive educational preparation and training;
2. an increasing vulnerability to the unauthorized practice of law;
3. an increasing vulnerability to professional liability in tort;
4. the growing demands for proof of continuing professional competence; and
5. the price of adherence to increasingly demanding codes of professional ethics.

A few of these costs will be borne more by insurance producers than they will be by other insurance practitioners. However, all insurance practitioners will pay a price, if they wish to reach and keep the heights of professionalism. They will pay for obtaining and maintaining high levels of competence and ethics, and they may, as Longfellow forewarned, be toiling upward in the night. Is it worth it? That is ultimately for each individual to decide. In so doing, perhaps each should remember that the best things in life are not always free.

CHAPTER 3

Codes of Professional Ethics

What gives the professional code its peculiar significance is that it prescribes also the duties of the members of a whole group towards those outside the group. . . . The attempt of professional groups to coordinate their responsibilities, relating at once the individual to the group and the group itself to the larger community, marks thus an important advance.
—R.M. MacIver

Most readers will probably be as surprised as the author was to discover the existence of such a large number of written codes of ethics. Indeed, in a 1972 survey of 1,800 national associations and societies, well over 350 were found to have such codes, and the number was beginning to grow rapidly.[52] To this one would have to add the countless number of ethics codes among individual business firms, governmental bodies, and labor organizations. In all, the total number of written ethics codes, in the United States alone, may well be in the thousands.

A prominent theologian and serious student of ethics, in assessing the future of ethics codes, made the following observation:

Today, although it is still a potent force, religion is fragmented and no longer can speak with a single voice. Furthermore, secularism is unquestionably taking a heavy toll of traditional religious values

---

52. See Robert Houston Smith, "New Directions for Ethical Codes," *Association and Society Manager,* December/January 1973-74, pp. 124-28. Dr. Smith is a Presbyterian minister and Fox Professor of Religion at the College of Wooster, Wooster, Ohio. He has already contributed much to the literature of ethics codes, and he is currently engaged in the writing of a comprehensive history of business ethics. In the early stages of developing a code of ethics for CPCUs, Dr. Smith provided some very valuable insights for those of us who were involved in the project. One always looks forward to the results of his scholarly research.

and sanctions. It is not implausible to see a concern to find a new, secular version of old religious strictures in the growing interest in ethical codes. Whether we like it or not, ethical codes are becoming the secular bibles of trades, professions, businesses, and avocations.

Association officials should not take these trends lightly. Ethical issues and the demand for public morality are not a passing fancy. Ethical codes are going to be with us for a very long time; they must be constantly changing in order to meet new moral problems and changing values within society.[53]

Although the author of these lines deserves the credit for pointing to secularism as a plausible reason for the renewed interest in ethics codes, many other authorities, some for different reasons, have come to very similar conclusions. Ethics codes are undoubtedly here to stay. But there are business executives, labor leaders, public officials, and professionals who will still need to be convinced that such codes ought to be sophisticated enough to address the complex ethical issues of the day.

It would be impossible even to list all the ethics codes in a volume of this length, much less to describe or analyze them. Some codes are volumes in themselves (e.g., the code of public accountants). In recognition thereof, this chapter necessarily will be devoted to a less ambitious task. After a brief review of various kinds of ethics codes, some commentary will be offered on the 'determinants of the ethical behavior of insurance practitioners. Most of the specific codes which will be mentioned are readily available for the asking, a few at a nominal price, and there is no shortage of published critiques on the codes of the recognized professions.

ETHICS CODES OF BUSINESS, GOVERNMENT, AND LABOR

The vast majority of large corporations have adopted codes or written standards of business ethics, as have most national trade associations. The code mandated by a 1957 labor convention became the code of every AFL-CIO affiliate. Additionally, there are numerous ethics codes at several levels of government. Governors have issued executive orders which promulgate ethics codes and apply them to state employees. Some of the state ethics codes extend to the faculty and staff of state-supported universities.[54] The nation's largest employer, the federal government, has adopted a variety of ethics codes. For instance, a 1965 Executive Order of President Johnson not only set forth broad standards of conduct

---

53. Ibid., at p. 128.
54. For further details, see *The Chronicle of Higher Education,* Vol. XII, No. 13, May 24, 1976.

for officers, employees, and advisors of the U.S. government; it also directed the Civil Service Commission to take the responsibility for making sure that each federal agency issued its own set of ethics standards. The Congress, as well as a number of state legislatures, also adopted codes of ethical conduct.

There is an endless supply of books and articles which advocate various notions of "corporate social responsibility" and "business ethics" or criticize the allegedly "unethical" nature of "capitalism" and "free enterprise." But the case for meaningful ethics codes has never been expressed more forcefully than it is in a recently published book, *The Ethical Basis of Economic Freedom,* edited by Ivan Hill.[55] In twenty-one fascinating chapters, each written by a distinguished leader in his field, the book explores the role of ethics in our society; ethics and honesty in law, medicine, accounting, government, organized labor, and transnational enterprises; the legal and enforcement aspects of ethics codes; and, the codes of ethics of the Direct Selling Association, the Public Relations Society of America, the National Association of Broadcasters, the American Society of Newspaper Editors, the National Association of Realtors, the American Football Coaches Association, and the International Association of Chiefs of Police. Throughout the book, the thread of connection among the chapters is that no new economic system is needed; rather, that human freedom can be preserved only if all citizens take the initiative to become more honest and ethical. There is also the unmistakable implication that many codes of ethics need to be strengthened.

In the meantime, the ethics codes of business, government, and labor too often contain standards which are neither honest nor ethical. Some codes do deal thoughtfully with issues such as public disclosure and conflicts of interest. Some are enforced and backed by severe penalties for violators. Others are little more than a collection of vague platitudes about the virtues of country, free enterprise, collective bargaining, or public service. Some codes address the crucial ethical issues of choice and priorities, whereas others read more like job descriptions than

---

55. Ivan Hill, ed., *The Ethical Basis of Economic Freedom,* "Plus special commentaries on Codes of Ethics and how they work," 1976, American Viewpoint, Inc., University Square, Chapel Hill, NC 27514. See also the earlier work of Henry Hazlett, "The Ethics of Capitalism," reprinted by the Education Division of the National Association of Manufacturers, 1965, from *The Foundations of Morality,* 1964, D. Van Nostrand Co., Inc. See also Milton Friedman, "Monopoly and the Social Responsibility of Business and Labor," *Capitalism and Freedom,* op. cit.; and Thomas A. Murphy, "A Businessman's Concern for Freedom" or Robert O. Harvey, "President's Newsletter" of Summer 1974, both published by Beta Gamma Sigma, St. Louis, MO.

ethics codes. Of course, as is true in the recognized professions, there are *individuals* in the business, government, and organized labor groups who live by the best qualities of professionalism. Nonetheless, in terms of an overriding concern for the broader public interest, one must reluctantly conclude that such groups, as a whole, do not yet compare favorably with some of the recognized professions.

ETHICS CODES OF RECOGNIZED PROFESSIONS

Theology

Most writers have presupposed that the clergy represent the very epitome of what is meant by professionalism. People frequently think of "religious" and "ethical" as synonymous terms, and they tend to regard the clergy as society's experts on what is right and wrong. Consequently, a member of the laity who questioned the personal ethics of the clergy has been traditionally thought of as sacreligious, at least by other members of the laity. Individual ministers, rabbis, and priests continue to be looked upon with reverential awe and respect, and deservedly so, by their peers, by their congregations, and by the laity and clergy of other religions. Yet, the personal ethics of the clergy as a whole are no longer beyond challenge.

In a recent survey conducted for a national newspaper, dozens of clergy, seminary teachers, ethicists, and members of the laity were reportedly interviewed.[56] Prominent Christian and Jewish theologians were quoted as saying that they are deeply concerned about such things as abuse of the laity's trust in order to satisfy the clergy's selfish needs, intellectual dishonesty to enhance theological opinions, irresponsible pandering or indoctrination in preaching, educational incompetence, the failure to develop professional skills, and the uncritical self-righteousness of too many clergy. Although one cannot be sure whether these views are representative of the inner concerns of the majority of the population, the more interesting revelation of this study, for our purposes, is that written codes of professional ethics for the clergy are apparently quite rare. The ministerial clergy are involved in highly visible occupations, of course, and they are subject to periodic evaluations by the laity, their peers, and their superiors in the organizational

---

56. The study, conducted for the *National Observer* by Dr. William J. Lanouette, is reported on in an article entitled "Study Finds Lack of Clergy Ethics Code; Tells Contemporary Concern," *National Catholic Reporter*, January 16, 1976, p. 15.

structures of their respective religions. But members of the clergy as a whole are not subject to a written ethics code that would be comparable, say, to the code which applies to practicing attorneys or public accountants. This is not to suggest that the theology profession is comparable to other occupations, or even that the clergy should have a common ethics code; it is merely to acknowledge that there is no overall ethics code to describe.

Medicine

The American Medical Association's "Principles of Medical Ethics" has been widely adopted throughout the various branches and specialties of the profession.[57] The AMA code is relatively brief, consisting of ten sections which provide general standards by which a physician may determine the ethical propriety of "his" [sic] conduct in relationships with patients, colleagues, members of allied professions, and the public. Particularly noteworthy are the two sections which obligate physicians to "make available to their patients and colleagues the benefits of their professional attainments," and to "expose, without hesitation, illegal or unethical conduct of fellow members of the profession." Nearly all of the other sections were reproduced or described in Chapter 1.

As also noted in Chapter 1, the AMA itself does not directly control the right to practice medicine. Such powers are vested in state boards of medical examiners, and specialty certifications are controlled by national medical specialty boards. Beyond the occasional loss of license one reads about, this author would only note that data on the enforcement of medical ethics have not been readily available to the lay public. However, the AMA has recently announced an interesting approach to public accountability. A National Advisory Committee on Ethics, which will function externally to the AMA, is to be composed of leaders from business, theology, law, and the academic community, including graduate students and deans.[58] The approach offers other professions some food for thought, particularly since physicians are consistently judged by the public to be among the most ethical of all professionals.

Even in a cursory review, one cannot leave the field of medicine without acknowledging the very difficult ethical issues which physi-

---

57. "Principles of Medical Ethics," op. cit., also reprinted in its entirety in Ivan Hill, *The Ethical Basis of Economic Freedom,* op. cit., pp. 173-74. The AMA code is sometimes adopted with annotations which are especially applicable to a particular specialty. One example is psychiatry, referred to in footnote 37, supra.
58. Ivan Hill, op. cit., pp. 10-11.

cians must deal with on a daily basis.[59] From an outsider's point of view, the modern ethical issues in medicine seem far too complex to be handled adequately by a code of ethics which prescribes only the broadest of principles to guide the physician, a code which has not been significantly revised in a number of years. Perhaps it is presumptuous for an outsider to judge how much professional independence is needed by physicians in order that they might best serve the public interest. One observes a seeming contradiction, though, in the trend toward further restrictions on the professional independence of members of other occupations which pose less complex ethical questions than the practice of modern medicine.

Law

The American Bar Association's Code of Professional Responsibility is a very elaborate code with many parts.[60] It was thoroughly revised in the late 1960s and subsequently adopted by all the enforcement agencies of the highest court in each state, though the enforcement rules and procedures are somewhat different in different states. The new Code consists of a "preamble," nine "canons," numerous "disciplinary rules," and numerous "ethical considerations." The nine *canons* are very brief statements of broad and axiomatic norms, general concepts from which the *ethical considerations* and *disciplinary rules* are derived. The *disciplinary rules* are mandatory in nature, expressing the minimum level of conduct below which a violator is subject to disciplinary action. The *ethical considerations* are aspirational objectives, statements of rationale, and guidelines for the application of specific rules. Violations of the specific *disciplinary rules* may lead to a private admonition, private reprimand, public censure, suspension, or disbarment. Various legal journals regularly publish summaries of the disciplinary actions which have been taken in a particular state.

Since merely to reprint the ABA Code standards would require over 100 pages, no analysis of them will be attempted here. Suffice it to say that the ABA Code has provoked much criticism, inside and outside the bar. Many contend that a lot of the rules for practicing attorneys are not really appropriate for lawyers who are employees of corporations and

---

59. For an inside look at the basic issues and how they are handled, see the analysis of Max H. Parrott, M.D., former president of the AMA, who authored the chapter on medical ethics in Ivan Hill, op. cit., pp. 161-72.

60. See footnote 32, supra. Also see Ivan Hill, ibid., pp. 175-95, for an analysis of honesty and ethics in the practice of law, authored by Leon Jaworski, Esq., a former ABA president who is perhaps best known to the lay public as the "Watergate" Special Prosecutor.

government agencies. Furthermore, some of the rules for practicing attorneys are felt to be unwarranted restrictions which are contrary to the public interest (e.g., restrictions on advertising and restrictions on specialization within the field of law). Nonlawyers also have ample reason to question whether the current boundaries defining the unauthorized practice of law are truly in the public interest, or whether they are just high-sounding disguises for self-serving protectionism. For instance, whereas real estate and insurance agents are prohibited from giving nearly any kind of legal advice to their clients (except to see a lawyer), many lawyers freely give real estate, insurance, and investment advice to their clients, without any proof of qualifications to do so. If legal restrictions on the unauthorized practice of law are in the public interest, as some restrictions undoubtedly are, should there not be legal restrictions on a lawyer's freedom to give advice on matters for which his law degree is hardly sufficient proof of qualifications and competence? Do ethics code restrictions on legal specialties weaken the bar's case for freedom to give the latter kind of advice? One at least has the legal right to wonder whether the *public* interest is adequately represented in the current ABA ethics Code.

Insofar as the interests of practicing attorneys and their clients are concerned, the strength of the ABA Code seems to lie in the specificity of its ethics rules. One may question some of the rules. Yet, if complex ethical issues are to be dealt with effectively, they cannot be circumvented by total reliance upon a small number of broad guidelines. They must either be dealt with specifically or left entirely to varying individual judgments of what is proper. Because the ABA Code gets specific, it is lengthy. Therein is a lesson which other organizations have yet to learn. They are content to tell their practitioners to "be ethical." They just have not told them what that really means, and in that sense they have missed the point.

Public Accounting

The Professional Standards of the American Institute of Certified Public Accountants are perhaps the most comprehensive and lengthy of all the recognized professions.[61] They likewise contain valuable notions which may be applied to other occupations, including insurance.

---

61. See the AICPA Professional Standards, op. cit. The current code, published in 1976, is a substantial revision of the earlier code. For two good explanations of the need for such a revision, see Willis A. Smith, "The Revised AICPA Rules of Conduct — To Serve the Public Interest," *The CPA Journal,* November 1973, pp. 963-68; and, Thomas G. Higgins and Wallace E. Olson, "Restating the Ethics Code: A Decision for the Times," *The Journal of Accountancy,* March 1972, pp. 33-39.

A single volume contains Concepts of Professional Ethics, Rules of Conduct, Interpretations of Rules of Conduct, Ethics Rulings and the Bylaws of the American Institute of Certified Public Accountants, i.e., four types of standards plus the Bylaws of the Institute. The *Concepts of Professional Ethics,* embodied in an essay approved by the professional ethics division, deal with independence, integrity, and objectivity; competence and technical standards; responsibilities to clients; responsibilities to colleagues; and other responsibilities and practices. These concepts are aspirational goals, not enforceable standards. The enforceable standards are contained in specific *Rules of Conduct.* The third category, *Interpretations of Rules of Conduct,* consists of rule interpretations which have been adopted as guidelines. Members who depart from these guidelines have the burden of justification in any disciplinary hearing. Members also have the burden of justifying departures from *Ethics Rulings,* which consist of formal rulings of the professional ethics division's executive committee. If all this is not enough, a member is also advised to consult ethical standards of the applicable state CPA society, state board of accountancy, the Securities and Exchange Commission (SEC), and similar government agencies. Perhaps accountants are accustomed to numbers. They certainly have a number of professional standards to observe.

Both the applicable standards and the disciplinary sanctions or penalties are complicated by the fact that there is an elaborate superstructure of societies, boards, and agencies which govern public accountants. The details are not important to this discussion. However, it is important to note that the penalties for ethics code violators range from the lesser sanctions, like reprimand, to the suspension, revocation, or withdrawal of the license to practice public accounting and/or the suspension or expulsion of membership in the AICPA and all state societies to which an accountant may belong. Despite the fact that the mere loss of CPA society membership does not necessarily preclude continued practice of a limited nature, it alone is considered a significant deterrent to unethical conduct; moreover, the CPA societies are inclined to refer serious code violations to the state licensing boards for consideration of license revocations. The AICPA also has established a program for referral of code violations to various agencies of the federal government.

The AICPA does not rely entirely on the ethics complaints received from the public or members of the profession. It also initiates investigations which are prompted by its monitoring of the financial press and litigation against its members. Investigations and disciplinary actions of the CPA societies are published only when a duly constituted Trial Board finds a member guilty of a code violation. However, available data show that the AICPA receives relatively few ethics complaints in relationship to the total membership, which now exceeds one hundred thousand. Of the cases concluded during the period 1970 to 1974, approximately 20 percent resulted in suspension or expulsion from AICPA membership, 35 percent resulted in censures, and 45 percent resulted in a finding of not guilty.[62] Comparatively few of the reported or discovered violations have involved fee disputes, dishonesty, lack of independence, or lack of professional competence. The majority of the complaints have involved conflicts between and among accounting practitioners, typically in the areas of encroachment on another's practice, solicitation of clients, indirect advertising, dual telephone listings, and similar practices. Some, while acknowledging the need for harmonious relationships among practitioners, have suggested that the public would benefit more from a relaxation of the code provisions dealing with the latter practices.[63]

The practice of public accounting involves various aspects which are unique among the recognized professions. First, since accounting is the language of business, the client is frequently as competent as the professional. The client is seeking primarily to add credibility to its financial statements in the eyes of third parties, and the client is normally in a much better position to judge the competence of an accountant than, say, a typical patient is able to judge the competence of a physician. Second, because the ultimate beneficiaries of the public accountant's services are third parties, the accountant needs independence *from* his client, unlike the advocacy role of a lawyer. Third, many accounting firms have become quite large, with as many as twenty thousand professionals in a single firm. Professional performance depends upon the firm's practices and policies, as well as upon personal characteristics of the professional. Fourth, public accountants are highly vulnerable to tort claims and litigation for civil damages. Part of this vulnerability stems from a widespread public misunderstanding of the inherent limitations of an audit. But a major part of it has to do with the potential consequences of an accountant's negligence. A physician's malpractice normally affects few persons and gets little public press. When a patient dies, the public does not necessarily presume that the death was caused by the attending physician's malpractice. When a major fraud is discovered and a large corporate enterprise becomes bankrupt, on the other hand, the natural tendency of the public is to presume negligence on the part of the accountant. In any event, the bankruptcy affects so many people that it invariably is reported in the mass communications media.

In spite of the unique demands placed upon public accounting prac-

---

62. See the chapter authored by C.E. Graese, CPA, chairman of the AICPA Ethics Division's Executive Committee, in Ivan Hill, op. cit., pp. 207-08.
63. Ibid., p. 208.

titioners, CPAs generally have earned the public trust by exhibiting high levels of professional competence, honesty, and ethical integrity. But one leader in the profession has been critical of the extent to which CPAs have been responsive to the broader needs of the public.[64] His examples include the failure of accountants to convey the limitations of an audit; the failure to update principles which have produced financial statements, in an inflationary economy, that are misleading to non-accountants; and, the failure, historically, to standardize and clarify "generally accepted accounting principles" to foster better public understanding of such principles. Some of these shortcomings are being discussed and dealt with, he concludes, but they continue to erode public confidence in the profession.

Some Implications

Though uncritical attempts to emulate the recognized professions can be self-defeating, all aspirants of professionalism have much to learn from the experiences of the recognized professions. Clearly, the absence of codes of ethics for the clergy is beginning to invite public criticism. Among the professions which do have written codes of professional ethics, all the codes have been criticized for (1) their preoccupation with the relationships between the professional and the professional's individual clients or patients, (2) their preoccupation with relationships between and among the professionals within a given occupation, and (3) their failure to deal adequately with the relationships between the professionals of a given profession and the members of other professions and occupations. These preoccupations and failures have led to the common charge that the recognized professions have not been sufficiently responsive to the broader interests and welfare of the general public. For example, the lay public is beginning to express its concerns about such things as physician strikes to protest rising malpractice insurance premiums, the rapidly rising costs of health care, the plaintiff attorneys' opposition to no-fault automobile insurance laws, the demonstrably greater emphasis on the rights of the accused than on the interests of victims and potential victims of crime, the treating of partisan political views as religious obligations, the lack of competition among professionals generally, and the vested interests of attorneys and accountants in the complicated tax laws, to mention just a few.

It also is instructive to speculate as to why the ethics of practicing physicians are still earning the esteem of the lay public, despite a broad and simple ethics code, whereas the ethics of practicing attorneys suffer

---

64. Ibid., pp. 209-13.

a tarnished image, despite the existence of numerous specific ethics rules. Accountants are subject to rigorous ethics rules *and* enforcement penalties, and public confidence in their competence and ethics stays high. And all of the recognized professions seem to be moving toward greater public accountability, if only to preserve their profession status.

Of all the recognized professions, however, aspirants of insurance professionalism probably have the most to learn from public accountants. Consider, for instance, a few of the similarities between insurance and accounting. Like the public accountant, the insurance professional frequently gives advice that may affect third-party beneficiaries, and the consequences of the insurance professional's negligence may likewise be severe. Many insurance practitioners also work for large insurance firms and, like some accountants, some insurance practitioners are not really engaged in "public practice." Some corporate insurance buyers are as sophisticated in insurance as corporate clients are in accounting, while some insurance buyers are not. The public is undoubtedly just as confused about "insurance principles" as they are about "generally accepted accounting principles" (and for about the same reasons). Insurance practitioners are apparently subject to more complaints about incompetence and dishonesty than accountants, but the ethics complaints about both occupations tend to be dominated by charges of "unfair competition" brought by one professional against another, rather than by complaints of professionals that there is not enough competition among them to benefit the public. There are also members of both occupations who live by the unwritten ethic of "thou shalt not knock thy competitor." Here, both groups just may have something to learn from medicine, where a physician is ethically obligated to *expose,* without hesitation, the incompetence of another physician (even though there is little economic competition among physicians).

There are other similarities between accounting and insurance, to be sure. The reader is free to add to the list or disagree with some of the suggestions made here. However, it is especially important to note some of the sharp *differences* between accounting and insurance *at the level of public practice.* At the level of public practice, i.e., at the level of dealing directly with individual members of the public in an advisory or service capacity, accountants and insurance practitioners share some common problems, but the similar problems are handled in a very different way. Compared to the public practitioners in insurance, the evidence confirms that *public accountants have been more responsive to public needs and interests,* and for the most part they have done so voluntarily (i.e., without waiting for government fiats). Specifically, CPAs have imposed the ethical obligation of independence, because they have been trying to protect public interests which go beyond the selfish interests of a client;

CPAs have pushed for mandatory continuing education for *all* public accountants, as a condition of the right to practice, because they have regarded such requirements as essential to the public interest; CPAs were nudged by the SEC and then adopted a voluntary peer review program; accountants created the Financial Accounting Standards Board, in the effort to clarify accounting "principles" for the benefit of the public; and, CPAs have started to talk about eliminating unwarranted restrictions on competition, again in the broader public interest more than the individual accountant's. It is true that the dominance of public accounting by CPAs gives the CPA societies much greater powers to effect such improvements than would the very limited powers of, say, the Society of CPCU or the various agents, brokers, and claims associations. And it is certainly true that some of the accountants' approaches to professional problems may not be equally appropriate for public practitioners in insurance. Yet, in trying to explain why public accountants have a better competence and ethics record, as well as a better image in the eyes of other recognized professions and the lay public, one may find a few answers in the greater efforts of accountants to respond to the needs and best interests of the *public* as a whole. Those may be fighting words. One hopes they will merely provoke thought.

ETHICS CODES FOR INSURANCE PRACTITIONERS

What are the various determinants of ethical behavior among insurance practitioners? As is true of any other occupation, the conscience of each individual ultimately determines the *upper* level of ethical behavior that each individual achieves and maintains. But what specific influences or forces determine the *minimum* levels of ethical behavior among insurance practitioners? In fact, what is "ethical behavior"?

Some Determinants of Minimum Ethics Standards

For the purposes of this essay, it does not seem necessary to explore all the philosophical meanings of ethics. Nor is it necessary or possible to make clear distinctions between ethics and morality, since they inherently overlap with one another. It is enough to recognize that "ethical" is another one of those "dialectical" terms, the general nature of which has already been discussed. What is "ethical" cannot be defined except in relation to what is "unethical." Furthermore, regardless of *who* draws the dividing lines between the two or *how* they are drawn, there will invariably be gray areas between ethical and unethical acts of omission or commission.

In the present context, "professional ethics" will be used simply to refer to the things which individuals should or should not do in the pursuit of their occupations. Who decides what "should" or "should not" be done in the practice of insurance? How is it decided?

Insurance practitioners are given a considerable amount of freedom to make individual judgments in the pursuit of their occupations. They may choose from a variety of jobs, most of which do not even require a license to practice. They are free to join or not to join various trade associations and professional societies. They are influenced by public and peer-group expectations, in varying degrees, yet CPCU or CLU designations are not preconditions of the right to practice, and such designations are not encouraged or demanded by many employers, associates, and clients.

The ethical behavior of insurance practitioners may also be influenced, in varying degrees, by the desire to make money, the compensation system they are under, the economic forces of competition, the threat of legal liability for professional negligence, their own moral and religious views, family expectations, financial troubles, emotional problems, the expectations of their bosses, the expectations of stockholders and/or policyholders, and many other influences. But insurance practitioners are not entirely free to define for themselves what is "ethical." If each person were totally free to "do his own thing," the *minimum* ethical behavior that is required would obviously be defined by the *least* ethical person in the group. Therefore, society has determined that protection of the larger public interest requires laws and regulations to govern the occupational conduct of insurance practitioners—to define, in other words, the minimum types and levels of professional conduct which may be engaged in without penalties from society as a whole. In that narrow sense, society determines what is professionally "ethical" for an individual to do or not to do.

The minimum standards of individual conduct, those prescribed by laws and regulations, have not satisfied most formal *groups* of insurance practitioners. Nor have such groups been satisfied with the nonlegal determinants of individual behavior. Part of this dissatisfaction stems from the knowledge that the potential penalties for violating laws and societal regulations do not prevent some individuals from breaking them. A significant part of the dissatisfaction of groups, however, is a dissatisfaction with the laws and regulations themselves. The rationale is again instructive. Even if the individual is always a law-abiding citizen, if each individual is allowed to define what is ethical within the boundaries of law, the minimum level of ethical conduct is, at best, defined by the law. Many insurance associations and societies are simply not satisfied with such implications. They want the group to define for individual members the types and levels of conduct which the group considers to be "ethical." Most (but not all) insurance associations and societies have tried to set their ethical minimums at much higher levels than would otherwise be required by law. All organizations which have succeeded have done so by adopting written codes of ethics.

Insurance Ethics Codes, Generally

Few readers will need to be reminded of the very large number of trade associations, societies and other organizations which are specifically for insurance practitioners. There are organizations for insurance agents, brokers, claims representatives, underwriters, safety engineers, managers, education and training directors, personnel and public relations directors, actuaries, defense attorneys, public loss adjusters, insurance buyers, and insurance women. There are local, state, regional, national, and international organizations. There are organizations for life insurers, property and liability insurers, health insurers, capital stock insurers, mutual insurers and fraternal societies, and separate organizations for producers in each category. There are organizations of reinsurers, statistical and rate-making organizations — and so on.

Many, many of the insurance organizations have written documents which they refer to as codes of ethics, as do many individual insurance companies. Some of the documents are truly codes of ethics. Others are not. A few of the organizations have broad powers to impose various disciplinary penalties or sanctions upon code violators, while most have only the ultimate sanction of expulsion from membership. Very few of the organizations have published written disciplinary rules and procedures, and fewer still have any direct control over certification or the right to practice insurance.[65] Beyond these broad observations, which were based upon a review of dozens of codes over the four-year period prior to this writing, no further description or analysis of them will be attempted.[66]

The remainder of this chapter will be devoted to a brief review of the

---

65. One partial but important exception concerns the relatively new "Certified Safety Professional" certificate (CSP). A board is given the authority to suspend, *refuse to renew or revoke the certificate of* any CSP, on such grounds as guilt of professional misconduct, incompetence, gross negligence, a felony or a crime involving moral turpitude, or obtaining a certificate through the use of fraud or deceit. The latter grounds are probably open to nearly any organization which issues certificates or degrees.

66. For an excellent discussion of many insurance organizations and their ethical principles, written some years ago by a CPCU, see Bernard John Daenzer, "Ethics and Insurance," *Ethics for Modern Business Practice*, J. Whitney Bunting, ed., 1953, Prentice-Hall, Inc.

respective ethics codes of the national CLU and CPCU societies, a quick look at "unfair insurance practices acts," and a few summary observations on ethics codes and the role of professionalism. The next and final chapter will summarize the development of the Code of Professional Ethics of the American Institute for Property and Liability Underwriters.

The American Society of CLU

The American Society of Chartered Life Underwriters has adopted a Code of Ethics for its members. The vast majority of CLUs are members of the Society and their own local chapter, but *membership* in the Society is not required as a precondition of the right to "practice" or the right to hold and use the CLU professional designation.

The American Society's Code of Ethics consists of eight Guides to Professional Conduct and six Rules of Professional Conduct. The *Guides* are broad standards which obligate members to place the welfare of clients above their own interests, provide clients with continuing service and counsel, continue to study and improve their technical competence, keep abreast of relevant changes and inform clients of such changes, develop good relationships with other professionals, avoid activities which would bring discredit upon the Society or the life insurance institution, and encourage other qualified individuals to earn the CLU designation. The *Rules* are more specific standards which obligate members to obey all life and health insurance laws, conduct their personal and business affairs in a way that will not discredit their reputations or the public regard for life underwriting, respect the confidential nature of the member/client relationship, respect the agency/principal relationship, avoid impairing the reputation or practice of another life underwriter, and advertise the CLU designation or its significance only in an officially approved manner.

The American Society of CLU has written "ethical guidance procedures" for chapters of the Society. Enforcement of the code is left primarily up to each local chapter. The local chapter receives all complaints, conducts hearings, and dismisses the cases or imposes penalties, all in accordance with elaborate procedural safeguards. A local chapter tribunal may reprimand a member (a formal rebuke given limited publication), or censure a member (a formal rebuke given wide publication), or dismiss the case, and such decisions may not be appealed to the American Society. However, a local chapter tribunal cannot suspend or revoke society membership. It can only recommend suspension or revocation to a national tribunal, which has the final say. A member is subject to the possibility of a disciplinary penalty for any code violation, whether a

Guide or Rule violation, but the tribunals are admonished to match the penalty with the severity of the misconduct (and a Rule violation would normally be a more serious type of misconduct). Based on the author's firsthand experiences as a member of the American Society and a member of several local chapters over the years, and confirmed through recent conversations with Society leaders, the author can safely make one valid generalization. Of the comparatively small number of alleged code violations reported, the majority involve charges made by one member against a competitor-member (usually an allegation of statutory "twisting" or of other unfair competitive practices).

The Society of CPCU

The Society of Chartered Property and Casualty Underwriters has adopted a Code of Ethics for its members. The vast majority of CPCUs are members of The Society of CPCU and their own local chapter, but *membership* in The Society is not required as a precondition of the right to "practice" or the right to hold and use the CPCU professional designation.

The (CPCU) Society's Code of Ethics was published in its entirety in a recent issue of the *CPCU Annals* (now called the *CPCU Journal*), as were the written disciplinary procedures.[67] However, a brief summary of the major code features should prove interesting to CPCU candidates, though they are not eligible for Society membership until they first have their CPCU designations conferred. (CPCU candidates may subscribe to the *CPCU Journal*, nonetheless, and they are encouraged to do so as a regular part of their CPCU studies.)

Structurally, The Society's Code of Ethics consists of seven "Specified Unethical Practices" and three "Unspecified Unethical Practices" of a more general nature. To paraphrase in the interest of brevity, the *Specified Unethical* Practices prohibit: violation of any law or regulation; willful misrepresentation or concealment of material facts; the breach of confidential relationships with clients or principals; willful misrepresentation of the nature or significance of the CPCU designa-

---

67. See Joseph P. Decaminada, CPCU, CLU, Chairman, Ethics Committee, Society of CPCU, "Code of Ethics of the Society of CPCU," *CPCU Annals,* Vol. 29, No. 3, September 1976, pp. 169-71. The Code is referred to in this article as a "proposed" code. However, the proposed code was subsequently adopted, by a wide margin, in a vote of the membership. See *CPCU News,* Vol. 25, No. 3, March 1977. The name of the *CPCU Annals* was changed, beginning with the March 1978 issue, to the *CPCU Journal.*

tion; unauthorized speaking or acting for the Society or a Chapter; aiding and abetting unethical practices; and violation of a Board directive to cease and desist. The *Unspecified Unethical* Practices obligate a member to: avoid practices which tend to discredit the Society or the insurance business; use diligence to ascertain the needs of a client or principal and avoid assignments which cannot be performed by the member in a professional manner; and use one's full knowledge and ability to perform duties for a client or principal.

The disciplinary procedures basically provide that, upon receipt of a written and signed request, The Society's president appoints a committee of inquiry to investigate. If the evidence so warrants, the president then appoints a three-member Conference Panel to hear the case. A *unanimous* opinion of the Panel is necessary to find an accused member's conduct to be unethical. If the Panel finds a member guilty of an "unspecified unethical practice," the president directs the member to cease and desist. (A member who does not oblige is thereby violating a specified unethical practice, as noted above.) If the Panel finds a member guilty of a "specified unethical practice," the Society's Board of Directors may reprimand, censure, suspend, or expel the violator from Society membership. Reprimands are reported only to the violator, whereas the other disciplinary sanctions are to be reported in the *CPCU News*. Unlike the CLU disciplinary procedures, all ethics complaints against members of The Society of CPCU are handled entirely at the national level. As of this writing, very few ethics complaints have been received by The Society.

It is important for the reader to remember that The Society of CPCU is a professional membership organization which only CPCUs are eligible to join. The Society is not required to accept all CPCUs into membership; it is free to set its own membership requirements, including compliance with its Code of Ethics. But every thoughtful CPCU certainly wants to join The Society and *actively participate* in the functions of The Society and its local chapters. Most members, including this author, feel a deep ethical obligation to support The Society and help it achieve the objectives which will ultimately benefit the public. Selfishly perhaps, if the reader will tolerate the obvious bias, one also treasures the priceless friendships with "the cream of the crop." If aspirants of professionalism are naturally fond of true professionals, does not the public ultimately benefit?

Finally, many CPCUs and CPCU candidates do not seem to fully understand that The Society of CPCU, as a professional membership organization, is a very different legal entity from the American Institute for Property and Liability Underwriters, Inc. The American Institute is a separate corporation in the nature of a nationwide college or educational institution. Members of The Society are "graduates" of the

Institute who meet The Society's membership requirements. But it is the American Institute which establishes the educational, experience, and ethics requirements which must be met and maintained for an individual to receive and keep the CPCU professional designation. As we will see in the next chapter of this essay, the American Institute has a written ethics code which is applicable to *all* CPCUs and CPCU candidates, whether or not they are members of The Society. It is used to screen applicants for CPCU candidacy and discipline CPCUs who violate the code. In serious cases, the Institute may suspend or revoke the privilege to use the CPCU professional designation in any way. Of course, The Society and the Institute are close relatives, *much* more so than the usual college-alumni relationship. Nearly all the Institute and Society professional staff are CPCUs who are members of the Society. Society leaders serve on the Institute's Board of Trustees, as well as on numerous Institute committees. Institute staff serve on Society committees and joint Institute-Society committees. And there is close liaison in every practical way, including a common location for the National headquarters of each organization. But the important thing to stress is that The Society and the Institute are legally separate entities. Each must abide by its own corporate powers, objectives, and authorities in conducting its activities, including ethics activities.

Unfair Insurance Practices Acts

There are two important reasons for considering "unfair insurance practices acts" in the context of insurance ethics codes. First, though they are directed largely at insurance institutions, the latest state acts have become significant determinants of the minimum ethical standards which are imposed upon insurance practitioners. Second, the acts of several large states impose more stringent and more specific standards than virtually every other written ethics code which has been voluntarily adopted by groups of insurance practitioners.

State insurance laws have been restrictive in nature for many years. Entry into the business has been controlled by the state licensing requirements for insurance companies, agents, and brokers.[68] A number of states also have occupational licensure requirements for insurance consultants and claims representatives. Furthermore, the power to suspend or revoke such licenses has long been used in the enforcement of state insurance statutes and regulations. And the laws themselves have

---

68. For a summary of occupational licensure requirements for producers, see George L. Granger, "State Licensing Requirements for Insurance Agents and Brokers," *CPCU Annals*, Vol. 27, No. 2, June 1974, pp. 128-36.

imposed numerous restrictions on the operational activities, functions, and practices of insurance companies and their representatives.

Recently, substantial changes in state insurance laws have imposed a lengthy list of additional restrictions on insurance practices. The newer laws began to surface with the announcement of a model bill developed by the National Association of Insurance Commissioners (NAIC). By the mid-1970s, a large number of states had enacted a new kind of unfair trade practices act. Much of the initial trade press coverage was devoted to the *claims* practices sections of the NAIC model bill, which prescribed fourteen specific claims practices that were to be deemed unfair and prohibited.[69] Some states adopted the model bill almost verbatim or added a requirement that insurers maintain a complaint register, while several larger states (e.g., New York and Illinois) adopted a much more comprehensive type of law. It soon became obvious that the state legislatures were beginning to make far-reaching increases in the scope and specificity of unfair insurance trade practices.

A dramatic case in point is provided by the Pennsylvania Unfair Insurance Practices Act of 1974, which is expected to be vigorously enforced.[70] The Act covers virtually every person and organization involved in nearly every kind of insurance and suretyship. It prohibits not only unfair methods of competition; it also prohibits unfair or deceptive acts or practices relating to: (1) sales techniques and marketing practices; (2) discrimination in rating and underwriting; (3) cancellation of policies; and (4) claims investigation and settlement.

The marketing section prohibits misrepresentations in any advertising which pertains to such things as the benefits, coverages, advantages, terms, dividends or descriptive titles of policies, or the financial condition of an insurer. It forbids the inducement of lapse, forfeiture, or cancellation of a policy by misrepresentations of fact; misrepresentation to get an assignment or loan on a policy; and misrepresentation of a policy as a share of stock. The Act forbids untrue, deceptive, or misleading statements regarding another practitioner or another practitioner's financial condition. It restates prohibitions against boycotts, coercion, monopoly, or other unreasonable restraints of trade. And it forbids the filing of false information in reports to State officials.

The Act contains sweeping prohibitions of discrimination. It pro-

---

69. The fourteen unfair claims practices, as well as additional requirements of several states, are described in Ralph W. Arnold, "Living with Unfair Claims Practices Acts," *Best's Review,* Property/Liability Edition, June 1975.

70. For an excellent analysis of this law by a knowledgeable Pennsylvania attorney, see Donald L. Very, Esq., "The Pennsylvania Unfair Insurance Practices Act: The Sleeping Giant," *CPCU Annals,* Vol. 28, No. 2, June 1975, pp. 109-16.

hibits discrimination between individuals of essentially the same hazard (or life expectancy) in premiums, fees, rates, or other contract provisions, except rates promulgated in compliance with rating statutes and regulations. In the area of underwriting, the Act forbids unfair underwriting practices or standards based upon race, religion, nationality, ethnic group, age, sex, family size, occupation, place of residence, or marital status. In addition, it generally prohibits the granting of special favors, such as rebates or special premiums.

The cancellation section extends the same sort of protection to owners of private residences and personal property as had been provided earlier for automobile policyholders. Generally, an insurer cannot cancel or refuse to renew homeowners or personal property coverages which have been in force for sixty days, except for nonpayment of premium, a material increase in hazard, or material misrepresentations or concealments at the time the policy was obtained. Extensive provisions relating to cancellation notices are also specified.

The section on claims investigation and settlement prohibits a lengthy list of specific practices which are deemed unfair. They forbid, for example, the misrepresentation of pertinent facts or contract provisions, forcing an insured to institute a lawsuit by offering an amount lower than that which is due, the failure to act promptly on written and oral communications, and the failure to attempt a fair settlement of a claim after the insurer's liability has become reasonably clear. The Act also forbids attempts to settle claims for less than the amount which a reasonable person would have believed he was entitled to receive, based on advertising circulars or information accompanying the application for insurance. Additionally, the Act prohibits the practice of failing to pay amounts due under one coverage in order to influence a settlement under another coverage or policy.

The penalties for violating the Act can be quite severe. Subject to judicial review, and after a hearing, the commissioner may order the violator to cease and desist (and seek a court injunction, if necessary). If it is a violation of section five of the Act, the commissioner may suspend or revoke the violator's license. In addition, if a person knew or should have known he was violating the Act, a civil penalty of $5,000 may be imposed for each violation. If the person did not know or reasonably should not have known of the violation, the penalty is reduced to a maximum of $1,000 per violation. But a fine of up to $10,000 may be imposed for violating an order issued by the commissioner. In short, violations may lead to cease and desist orders, loss of license, and/or heavy fines.

It is not yet clear whether other states will enact unfair insurance practices laws which are as extensive in scope and specificity as the

Pennsylvania Act. However, in the area of claims practices, at least, the new statutes clearly have imposed a number of more demanding standards, as well as stronger disciplinary penalties, than the existing ethics codes of most insurance associations, societies, and membership organizations. This fact of life would seem to pose several awkward ethical dilemmas for membership organizations. Their written ethics codes invariably urge members to obey all laws and regulations pertaining to insurance. Yet, there are provisions of the new unfair trade practices acts which thoughtful people believe to be contrary to the public interest. If membership organizations try to get such provisions changed, perhaps they will be vulnerable to charges of self-serving political lobbying of an unprofessional nature, as indeed the American Medical Association was in its opposition to medicare; or, at a minimum, they probably will have the burden of proving that such changes would be in the larger public interest. If membership organizations do not expel members who violate existing insurance laws, on the other hand, they will surely be accused of having lower ethical standards than the laws proscribe.

A related dilemma concerns the matter of occupational licensure. Most of the membership organizations have no direct control over the licensing of insurance practitioners.[71] In fact, the various insurance professional societies have thousands of members whose occupational positions are not subject to any state licensing requirements. For good reasons, the professional societies, as entities, have resisted the temptation to engage in political lobbying. (Some even forbid it in their bylaws and/or ethics codes.) Some insurance company and producer organizations do have considerable political power, but they are by no means united in their views on occupational licensure. While some producers' associations have been successful in strengthening the educational preconditions for obtaining an agent's or broker's license, they have not infrequently done so by prevailing over the solid opposition of individual insurers and insurer associations. Moreover, some producers' associations have supported the kinds of licensing requirements which critics feel are in the nature of unwarranted restrictions on entry and competition. It is interesting, too, that producer and company associations do not seem inclined to propose or support licensing requirements for underwriters, investment specialists, rate-making specialists, company

---

71. It is noteworthy that several states now exempt CLUs and CPCUs from the necessity of taking all or portions of the state licensing exams for insurance producers. However, the exemption does not stem from membership in their respective societies; it is a privilege granted to holders of the designations, even if they are not society members.

executives, state insurance department employees, or other insurance practitioners, despite the well-known fact that an incompetent chief executive, say, could do far more harm to the general public than an individual agent. So also could thousands of people be harmed by even one bad decision of an incompetent underwriter, investor of policyholder premiums, or state insurance commissioner. What is probably even more important to the public interest, however, is the fact that producer and company associations have shown little interest in proposing or supporting more meaningful *ethics* preconditions for occupational licensure.

In raising such issues, the author does not wish to imply simple solutions. Nor does he wish to imply that the public interest would be better served by total insurance industry agreement on the solutions. To the contrary, a diversity of viewpoints, honestly and vigorously expressed by insurance professionals, may do far more to clarify the underlying issues than all of the so-called "consumer advocates" have done to date. What all the diverse factions of the insurance industry must learn to agree upon, it would seem, is the critical need to put the *public* interest above those of the other occupational interests which are entirely self-serving. Having first agreed on that much, insurance professionals can then get on with the even more difficult task of defining the "public interest" in specific terms. To leave this task entirely in the hands of partisan politicians and demagogues is to run the risk of losing another degree of precious human freedom, with results that do not even promise the consolation of having served the common good.

The most common reaction to increasing political problems is to urge increasing political involvement. Insurance trade associations have urged their members to join together in group-sponsored political action committees and paid lobbyists. Insurance professional societies have urged their members to become politically involved as individual citizens. At meetings and seminars of trade associations and professional societies, speakers endlessly summon their audiences to become "politically involved," so as to prevent a wholesale takeover of private insurance by the government. Lovers of smaller government and larger freedom can easily appreciate both the objective and the means of accomplishment. Political apathy is dangerously widespread, as is the growing tendency of the citizenry to look to government for solutions to all social problems. Nonetheless, why do so many speakers save their political involvement messages until after things like unfair insurance practices acts have been proposed or enacted? Would such laws ever get proposed or enacted if all insurance practitioners lived by higher standards of professional ethics? Would such laws get enacted if insurance organizations had and enforced ethics codes which paid relatively more attention to their ethical obligations to the public?

INSURANCE ETHICS CODES AND PROFESSIONALISM

One struggles with the question of whether the public interest would be better served if trade associations and/or professional societies had more direct controls over the occupational licensure of insurance practitioners. Even so, one can warm up quickly to the broader hope that membership organizations will adopt meaningful ethics codes, strengthen their sanctions, and make membership a valuable privilege. One also finds great comfort in the apparent spread of insurance professionalism, individuals who seek to maintain high ethical standards, not out of a fear of government intervention alone, but out of a larger sense of what is inherently right and wrong.

Intelligent and sensitive insurance professionals are beginning to make substantial progress in defining the public interest *in a way which will truly benefit the public.*[72] They are cutting through the arrogant advocacy by misguided demagogues of superficial notions about "corporate social responsibility," "consumerism," "free enterprise," and the so-called "unethical nature of profits and capitalism." True professionals reject the path of least resistance. They are speaking out, taking sides. They understand why they view self-styled "consumer advocates" with ambivalence. They welcome the publicly stated objectives of consumer advocates; they at once now appreciate the dangers of allowing the public interest to be defined by those whose motives or interests are essentially political. Unfortunately, too many insurance practitioners do not seem to be listening to the true professionals. Too many practitioners continue to acquiesce to what they perceive as the "political realities" of our times. Perhaps they are not paying enough attention to public opinion polls. Perhaps they are paying too much attention to

---

72. For some excellent examples of how true professionals can penetrate through the surface of things to address the real public interest questions in insurance, see William G. Pritchard, Jr., CPCU, "Social Responsibility in the Insurance Marketplace," *CPCU Annals,* Vol. 27, No. 1, March 1974, pp. 46-48; Denis A. Cleaver, CPCU, "Consumerism to Destruction? A Company Man's View," *CPCU Annals,* Vol. 27, No. 4, December 1974, pp. 322-23; and in the September 1974 issue of the *CPCU Annals,* also give careful reading to Dr. John D. Long, CPCU, CLU, "Social Responsibility of Insurance Companies: A Point of View," James S. Kemper, Jr., "Business Accountability for Social Action," and Stan Fish, CPCU, "Keep the Renaissance Moving." See also the most interesting research results of Lawrence G. Brandon, CPCU, "Value Orientations of Insurance Industry Chief Executives: A Study of the Identification and Role of Personal Values in Decision Making," *CPCU Annals,* Vol. 29, No. 3, September 1976, pp. 205-12.

them. Before jumping to the hasty conclusion that the two preceding sentences are contradictory, let us first look briefly at public opinion.

Life insurance industry organizations use scientific samples and studies to monitor the opinions of life insurance consumers on a regular and continuing basis.[73] According to the results of statistically reliable surveys, almost 90 percent of the heads of households feel it is more important to select a life insurance company carefully than it is to select a salesperson. They want their companies to be strong and reliable, and they tend to judge strength and reliability by the company's size and age. When in the market for life insurance, 40 percent of the people now say they would get in touch directly with the company.

About 75 percent of the adult consumers resent being contacted by a life insurance agent unless they are in the market for coverage. Some 67 percent feel that life insurance agents' recommendations are affected by the commission system, though 64 percent feel that the services provided by life insurance agents are worth any additional costs which the commission system entails. They place particular value on the information, explanations, and personal attention of their agents. Compared to earlier surveys, public opinion of life insurance agents had sharply improved, by 1976, in favor of the agents. Resentment of life insurance agents seems to have more to do with the guilt feelings they create than it does with the commission system or to high pressure sales techniques. Now that several of the largest life insurers are aggressively marketing automobile and homeowners insurance, one wonders whether the overall public opinion of life insurance agents will continue at the same rate of improvement. The property and liability segment of the insurance industry does not get a good report card from the general public.

In a recent survey of public attitudes, *U.S. News & World Report* asked people to rate thirty-one industries on the basis of their overall performance.[74] In terms of the number of respondents who gave good

---

73. For examples, see "Life Insurance Consumers," A Review of the Literature by the Life Insurance Agency Management Association (LIAMA) in Cooperation with The Institute of Life Insurance (now the American Council of Life Insurance or ACLI), LIAMA Research Report 1973-10, file No. 940. This report contains major findings of periodic surveys conducted by such organizations as LIAMA, ACLI, the Life Underwriter Training Council (LUTC) and a number of mass-circulation magazines. Most of the information referred to above was taken from a 1976 ACLI survey, "Monitoring Attitudes of the Public," made available to the author through the courtesy of the Council.

74. The "Insurance Educators Letter" reports that single copies of this study are available from the Director of Marketing, *U.S. News & World Report,* 2300 N. Street, N.W., Washington, D.C. 20037. It is a second annual survey of public attitudes entitled "The Study of American Opinion."

ratings on "overall performance," property and casualty insurers ranked twenty-fifth out of the thirty-one industries rated. Medical and hospital insurers ranked twenty-sixth. Auto insurers ranked twenty-ninth. Only 16 percent of the respondents gave good overall performance ratings to property and casualty insurers, while only 12 percent gave good ratings to auto insurers.

The Opinion Research Corporation has a good reputation for accuracy in its periodic nationwide surveys of the adult public. In 1974, the OPR published a fascinating profile of how consumers view the insurance industry.[75] Insurance agents were regarded favorably by 52 percent of the people, yet 32 percent had "mixed" feelings, and another 12 percent had negative feelings about insurance agents, thus placing them well below the comparable ratings for doctors, bankers, and lawyers (and only slightly above real estate agents). The difficulty in collecting on claims led the list of specific complaints against property-casualty companies. Overcharging was a distant second. Even so, when people were asked to select products or services which give them the *least for their money,* auto insurance was near the top of the list, exceeded only by groceries, cosmetics and toiletries. The impression is likewise widespread that business profits are in excess of 25 percent of sales, an error of fact which no doubt led two-thirds to feel that business has a moral obligation to help society, even if it means dipping into profits. The percent of people who think new federal laws are necessary to help them get better value for their shopping dollars has grown each year, so that 66 percent favored new federal laws by 1971.

How do people perceive the ethical and moral practices of insurance companies generally? By 1974, some 15 percent of the adult population cited life insurance *companies* for poor ethical and moral practices, whereas 13 percent gave poor ethics ratings to property-casualty companies. If that is not discouraging enough, consider the fact that the few companies who got worse ratings included auto dealers, advertisement agencies, and television networks. Of course, these are only people's impressions, not necessarily the facts. But public impressions are no less a part of the real world in which the insurance industry operates.

The evidence suggests that some insurance practitioners have totally ignored the reliable public opinion polls. A larger number seem to have overreacted with hasty conclusions. To ignore public opinion altogether is to contradict the claim of serving public needs and interests; to overreact is to confuse the majority opinions of the masses with eternal truths. Ironically, both mistakes can foster laws and regulations

---

75. See John S. Schafer, Vice President, Opinion Research Corporation, "American Insurance: The Consumer's View," *CPCU Annals,* Vol. 27, No. 2, June 1974, pp. 143-47.

which are not in the overall public interest.

For the sake of argument, let us suppose there are 100 million adults in the population, of which only the tiny fraction of 500 thousand are knowledgeable insurance professionals. Assume further that a representative sampling of opinion was taken from the 99.5 million adults who are not insurance professionals. How would the vast majority of nonprofessionals feel about the advisability of national health insurance, no-fault auto insurance, open competition in rating, the commission system for compensating agents and the contingent fee system for compensating plaintiffs' attorneys? How would they evaluate: the effect of products liability losses on the retail prices of products and the effect of malpractice losses on the price of hospital and medical care; the relative importance of long-term disability insurance, major medical expense insurance, and term life insurance; the advisability of rigid auto drivers' license requirements to weed out irresponsible motorists, assigned risk plans and merit rating; the social desirability of life insurers' investing billions of dollars in urban core housing projects, the money spent on institutional advertising, and the money individual insurers contribute to colleges and universities; and the prospects for lowering the cost of insurance by having the federal government take over the industry? Would the majority opinions of nonprofessionals provide answers which would be in the overall public interest? Is it not possible that the collective opinions of competent and ethical insurance professionals would hold greater promise for defining what best serves the public at large?

One could go through a similar exercise concerning the written ethics codes in law, medicine, accounting, and insurance. The masses probably would agree with their general emphasis on honesty and integrity. Even so, would the majority opinions of the lay public be the best determinants of specific rules in codes of professional ethics? Should the matter be entrusted to legislators and insurance regulators? The author has forgotten the name of an Indiana philosopher who said something like this: "Civilization is in danger when those who have never learned how to obey are given the right to rule." Perhaps his notion has applicability to insurance legislators, regulators, and the majority of consumers. It could conceivably apply, as well, to some of the leaders of insurance trade associations and professional societies.

Whether one likes it or not, written codes of professional ethics are probably here to stay. If so, every insurance professional should assist in improving the codes in a fashion which gives the highest priority to serving the overall public interest. Every true professional will voluntarily observe the minimum levels of ethical conduct and aspire to much higher levels, not so much out of a threat of penalty for violation or a fear that the government would otherwise impose more restrictive standards. The true professional does so from a deep sense of knowing that some conduct is proper simply because it is proper. That, indeed, is what professional ethics is all about.

CHAPTER 4

The American Institute's Code of Professional Ethics

*It is a piece of idle sentimentality that truth, merely as truth, has
any inherent power denied to error, of prevailing . . . . The real
advantage which truth has consists in this, that when an opinion is true it may be extinguished once, twice, or many times,
but in the course of ages there will generally be found persons to
rediscover it, until some one of its reappearances falls on a time
when from favorable circumstances it escapes persecution until
it has made such head as to withstand all subsequent attempts
to suppress it.*
—John Stuart Mill

The American Institute for Property and Liability Underwriters is a
nonprofit educational institution which received its corporate charter
from the Commonwealth of Pennsylvania in 1942. The primary purpose
of the Institute is to establish and administer professional standards so
that properly qualified persons may be recognized with the professional
designation, Chartered Property Casualty Underwriter (CPCU). The
privilege to use the CPCU designation is conditioned upon the meeting
and maintaining of prescribed standards of professional competence and
ethics.

All applicants must complete the matriculation form, provide proof
of high school graduation or its equivalency, agree to abide by the Code
of Professional Ethics, agree to various other conditions, and be
screened by the Board of Ethical Inquiry. Applicants who meet these
requirements are admitted to CPCU candidacy. Thereafter, candidates
are eligible to take the ten national examinations which are prescribed,
but they may not use the CPCU designation until they (1) pass all ten
examinations, (2) offer proof of three years of acceptable insurance
experience, and (3) have their CPCU designations officially conferred by

the Institute. If a candidate is found guilty of violating a Rule of Professional Conduct, his or her CPCU designation may be withheld indefinitely, or until convincing proof of full and complete rehabilitation is furnished, even if such candidate has met the initial matriculation, examination, and experience requirements. Once the CPCU designation is conferred, the privilege to use it is conditioned upon continued compliance with the Rules of Professional Conduct which are set forth in the Code of Professional Ethics. Among other things, the Rules obligate the CPCU to keep informed on those matters that are essential to the maintenance of the CPCU's professional competence. Violation of any Rule may subject the violator to the possibility of disciplinary action, including the suspension or revocation of the privilege to use the CPCU professional designation in any way.

The Code of Professional Ethics was approved by the American Institute's Board of Trustees on June 18, 1976. All CPCU candidates are required to demonstrate their understanding of the Code and Code-related materials, which have been incorporated into the study assignments and examination questions for CPCU 10. Although the Code and the Code-related materials are printed in a separate volume, this chapter is devoted to some background information which should make it easier for candidates to appreciate and understand the rationale of the Code, the Guidelines for Professional Conduct, the Disciplinary Rules, Procedures and Penalties, and the published Advisory Opinions of the Board of Ethical Inquiry.

THE NEED FOR A COMPREHENSIVE CODE

Despite the fact that the founding fathers of the American Institute emphasized professional ethics from the very beginnings of the CPCU designation the only written ethics standards, for the first thirty-two years, took the form of a so-called "CPCU Professional Charge," the latest revision of which is as follows:

> In all my business dealings and activities, I agree to abide by the following rules of professional conduct:
> I shall strive at all times to ascertain and understand the needs of those whom I serve and act as if their interests were my own; and, I shall do all in my power to maintain and uphold a standard of honor and integrity that will reflect credit on the business in which I am engaged.

An adaptation of the Golden Rule, the "charge" was the CPCU's counterpart to the physician's Hippocratic oath. At every national conferment exercise and local diploma presentation ceremony, all new designees, along with all CPCUs who were present, stood and raised their right hands, repeating the Charge aloud. It was a proud moment for all.

The impetus for a new code of ethics was provided by a massive revision of the entire CPCU curriculum. In the early part of 1974, your author was asked to write a documented "position paper" on what the role of professional ethics should be in the new CPCU curriculum. After much study of the literature and lengthy correspondence and consultations with prominent theologians, fellow CPCUs, and representatives of the national ethics committees of all the recognized learned professions, it was eventually decided that every CPCU candidate should be required to engage in a rigorous study of professional ethics. Accordingly, the first step would be to develop a comprehensive written code of professional ethics, supplemented by newly-written study materials with intellectual substance. The CPCU Charge was not enough. Serviceable as it had been as a lofty commitment to ethics, it was not specific enough to meet the Institute's objectives and otherwise address the growing complexities of ethical choices in modern society.

DEVELOPMENT OF THE CODE

Having already formulated its ethics-related objectives, the Institute first sought to develop a code of ethics by initiating a joint effort with the Ethics Committee of the Society of CPCU. This effort spanned the period from February 1974 to March 1975, at which time the Society elected to pursue the matter independently. Both organizations had become acutely aware of their differing scopes and legal powers. The Society is a membership organization, as noted earlier. It has jurisdiction only over its members, and its ultimate sanction is to expel a person from membership. The American Institute has jurisdiction over all CPCUs, including those who are not Society members, and it has the legal authority to confer and revoke the privilege to use the CPCU designation. Careful attempts were made to assure that the Society's ethics code would not conflict with the Institute's, that there would be close liaison between the two organizations, and that each would work toward the eventual consolidation of the two codes. In the meantime, the Society wanted to bring to an early conclusion the efforts which had already taken them years, whereas the Institute had just gotten started, and it seemed unlikely that it would be able to get an ethics code developed and approved for some time. (The Institute Code was later developed and approved in a much shorter period than most thought possible, yet few had anticipated that this would happen.)

The Institute Task Force

To carry forward the work undertaken during the previous two years and bring the ethics project to a satisfactory conclusion in time to meet the established deadlines of the new CPCU curriculum, the Institute formed a new ethics "Task Force" in June 1975. The major components of the Task Force were as follows:

1. The American Institute's "Ad Hoc Committee on Professional Ethics," appointed by the President with the advice and approval of the Chairman of the Board of Trustees.[76]
2. "The Ethics Policy Committee" of the American Institute's Board of Trustees, appointed by the Chairman of the Board.
3. Outside Legal Counsel
4. The Board of Trustees of the American Institute[77]

The "Ad Hoc Committee" was charged with the responsibilities of conducting the necessary research, drafting a code of ethics, and preparing formal recommendations for the consideration of the "Ethics Policy Committee," which in turn was to report and make recommendations to the Executive Committee and the full Board of Trustees.

Ethics Objectives

During the two years prior to the establishment of the Task Force, countless hours had been devoted to the formidable but highly essential

---

76. Members of the Ad Hoc Committee were Dr. Edwin S. Overman, CPCU, Dr. Glenn L. Wood, CPCU, CLU, Dr. Frederick R. Hodosh, CPCU, Warren T. Hope, M.A., Lawrence G. Brandon, CPCU, Dr. Evan E. Clingman, CPCU, Dr. Norman A. Baglini, CPCU, Dr. George L. Head, CPCU, CLU, Margaret A. Kelley, CPCU, CLU, Dr. John D. Long, CPCU, CLU and Dr. Ronald C. Horn, CPCU, CLU (Committee Chairman).
77. Although the membership of the Board changes each year, the members and their positions are listed in the yearly editions of the *IIA/CPCU Catalog*. Ex Officio members of the Board include the President of the Institutes, the President of the Society of CPCU and the Executive Vice President of the Society. Numerous other Society leaders are members of the Institute Board. At the time the Code was approved, the members of the Ethics Policy Committee were: Melvin A. Holmes, CPCU, Committee Chairman, Vice Chairman of the Board, Frank B. Hall & Co.; Harold A. Eckmann, Chairman and Chief Executive Officer, The Atlantic Companies; and Porter Ellis, CPCU, Ex Officio (as Chairman of the Institute's Board of Trustees), Ellis Crotty Powers & Co. Outside legal counsel was provided by the law firms of Lamb, Windle & McErlane, West Chester, PA, and Webster & Chamberlain, Washington, D.C.

task of formulating the precise objectives and needs of the American Institute in the area of professional ethics. The Institute's long-standing broad objective was (and is) to *foster ethical conduct* on the part of CPCUs and CPCU candidates. This broad objective served as the basis for more specific objectives in the three areas identified below.

A. *Educational*   First and foremost, the Institute developed educational objectives and gave them high priority in the revised CPCU curriculum. Three full assignments in CPCU 10 were allocated to the subject of professionalism and professional ethics. For this ethics segment, the CPCU Curriculum Committee approved the following specific educational objectives:

"Every CPCU candidate should be required to demonstrate an intellectual ability to:

1. synthesize and explain the rationale by which CPCUs are obligated, to the insuring public, to other CPCUs, to the industry, and to themselves, to observe high standards of professional ethics;
2. recognize, recall, illustrate, and analyze what lawyers, physicians, CPAs, and other professionals have done to prescribe and enforce standards of ethical conduct for members of their respective professions, and evaluate the desirability of such activities for CPCUs;
3. recognize and evaluate the adequacy of such standards for ethical conduct as are prescribed or provided for insurance practitioners by laws, regulatory agencies, competition and economic influences, peer group pressures, expectations of the public, and other similar determinants of the outside boundaries of ethical conduct;
4. recognize, analyze, and evaluate the potential consequences of unethical conduct, not only for the individuals directly involved but for other larger entities and institutions;
5. explain the rationale by which each and every individual CPCU must bear the ultimate responsibility for his (her) own ethical behavior, if the highest standards of professional ethics are to prevail;
6. paraphrase, illustrate, explain, and apply to specific case situations the Code of Professional Ethics approved by the American Institute; and
7. distinguish between and among practices which are regarded as clearly unethical, clearly ethical, and questionably ethical for CPCUs to engage in, and explain the rationale by which such practices have been so classified by the Board of Ethical Inquiry."

To achieve the educational objectives, this essay was published by the Institute and assigned as reading material for all CPCU candidates. To achieve the objectives numbered 6 and 7 above, it was also essential to have an Institute board-approved Code of Professional Ethics, as well as written Guidelines, Case Studies, and formal Opinions which would be applicable to the wide variety of occupational positions which CPCUs hold. These latter materials were published in a separate volume, along with the approved Disciplinary Rules, Procedures, and Penalties, and assigned for reading and study by CPCU candidates. The two volumes were tailored to match the specified objectives and provide a sound foundation for the structuring of meaningful examination questions, questions of the same depth and overall quality as are fashioned for all of the other subject matter in the CPCU curriculum.

B. Screening of CPCU Candidates   Second, the Institute has always had the objective of conferring the CPCU designation only on those who have met the Institute standards pertaining to knowledge, experience, and *professional ethics*. Historically, a Registration Committee had the responsibility of evaluating the ethical qualifications of all CPCU candidates, both at the time they first applied for candidacy and again just prior to approval of the conferment of designations. Comparatively few candidates had been charged with ethical improprieties, but the resolution of the cases had often been troublesome. The Registration Committee needed, beyond the CPCU Charge, more explicit standards against which to judge the alleged ethical improprieties of CPCU candidates.

The Institute staff also felt a strong moral obligation to provide candidates with the explicit ethics standards they would be required to meet. It seemed grossly unfair to allow candidates to pay fees and pass all the examinations, only to have a few told that they had not met some vague and unspecified ethical standards. Additionally, the courts of law were beginning to challenge the legality of disciplinary procedures and other ethics activities of recognized professions. The Institute legal advisors had felt, historically, that the Institute was a unique educational entity which would not fall under the law concerning professional societies, associations, and membership organizations. However, recent court decisions had underscored the need to review all the legal implications of the Institute's increasing involvement in professional ethics activities.

C. Maintenance of Ethical Standards Among CPCUs   Third, the Institute had the objective of taking a more active role in the maintenance of ethical standards among those who already hold the CPCU professional designation. The Institute did not intend to plunge hastily into the role of policeman or judge. It did not intend to impose unreasonably strict standards, and it did not intend to impose harsh penalties on everyone found guilty of ethical misconduct. The Institute did (and does) feel obligated to the general public, as well as to all ethical CPCUs, to make sure that the integrity of the designation is preserved in a reasonable manner.

Of these three broad categories, it bears repeating that the *educational* objectives are by far the most important and immediate concern of the American Institute. The deliberations eventually led to the conclusion that a "good" code of ethics could be used to satisfy all three sets of institutional objectives, *provided that,* wherever there is a conflict between and among the categories, the educational objectives would be overriding. *The ultimate goal is to foster a high level of ethical conduct on the part of all CPCUs and CPCU candidates.* To that end, the Institute's primary role is to remove the intellectual barriers to ethical conduct. The enforcement aspects are simply a necessary part of preserving the integrity of the code and the CPCU designation.

Code Attributes

Once the objectives had been formulated and approved, the next step was for the Ad Hoc Committee to translate the objectives into operational criteria that could be used to design a "good" code for Institute purposes. That is to say, a "good" code for Institute purposes would have "attributes" that would enable the Institute to achieve its objectives satisfactorily. The following is a very brief summary of the attributes which were agreed upon.

A "Good" Code of Ethics (for Institute Purposes) Should:
1. be educational and inspirational;
2. provide practical guidance for those subject to the Code;
3. place primary emphasis on the public interest;
4. deal adequately with conflicts of interest;
5. avoid protectionism, possible antitrust problems, and self-serving language;
6. contain no language intended solely to enhance the public relations image of CPCUs or the Institute;
7. be generally acceptable to those subject to the Code;
8. be legally enforceable by the Institute (within reason);
9. be as simple as possible but comprehensive in scope;
10. be accompanied by a statement of rationale, definitions, and intent;
11. be applicable to a wide variety of real-world situations;

12. be applicable to business and professional conduct (rather than personal conduct per se);
13. be accompanied by interpretations, guidelines, disciplinary rules, and case studies;
14. contain several kinds of standards so as to accommodate the critical need for different degrees of specificity in the achievement of multiple objectives which would otherwise be conflicting;
15. avoid sexist language;
16. apply to the wide variety of occupational positions which CPCUs hold; and
17. be acceptable to the Institute's Ethics Policy Committee, Executive Committee, and Board of Trustees.

Some of these attributes inherently conflict with one another. For example, it is nearly impossible to have a brief and simple code and still have standards which are specific and comprehensive enough to be educational, provide practical guidance for those subject to the Code, apply to a wide variety of real-world situations, and apply to the wide variety of occupational positions which CPCUs hold. Standards which are specific and reasonable enough to be enforceable lose almost all of their inspirational value, and so on. Thus, to achieve all of the objectives, it was necessary for the Code to have several different types of standards. Specific rules would be used to prescribe the minimum and enforceable standards. Broader standards would also be used, because of the desire to make the Code more educational, more inspirational, and more comprehensive in scope. The enforceable rules would *mandate the desired minimum levels of conduct;* the other standards would *encourage a striving for desirable levels of conduct well beyond the minimums.* Yet, since some of the attributes would still conflict with others, an elaborate weighting scheme was used to rank them in order of importance. Suffice it to say that the highest priority was given to those attributes which relate directly to the *educational* objectives. Notions like brevity and legal enforceability would be sacrificed, whenever necessary, to achieve the educational goals.

There are many ways to structure a code of ethics.[78] Many organizations make the common mistake of trying to draft the code language without first reaching agreement on their objectives. Consequently, what appear to be arguments about the length, specificity, and format of

---

78. Organizations which face the task will find some good ideas in Eileen Creamer O'Neill, "Creating and Promoting a Code of Ethics," *Association Management,* November 1972, pp. 44-50; and Robert Houston Smith, "New Directions for Ethical Codes," *Association and Society Management,* December/January 1973-74, op. cit.

the code are not that at all. They are rather just an inevitable result of the fact that the proponents and opponents have very different (and unspecified) objectives in mind.

The Ad Hoc Committee spent many laborious hours in specifying and weighting the various objectives of the Institute. Only then did it set about to reach agreement on the code language. One cannot meaningfully evaluate the quality of *any* ethics code except in relation to specified and prioritized objectives. It is a "good" code to the extent that it meets the more important objectives. It is a "bad" code to the extent that (1) the objectives are not made explicit, (2) the relative importance of the objectives is not made explicit, (3) the code does not satisfactorily meet the specified objectives, and/or (4) the objectives themselves are deficient. Specifying the objectives at the outset permits initial and subsequent evaluation of the code standards and the objectives they are designed to meet.

Problems and Issues

Initial drafts of the code, along with related recommendations, were submitted to the Ad Hoc Committee in mid-1975. Subsequently, a painstaking editorial process involved twenty-six all-day meetings of the Ad Hoc Committee, two all-day joint meetings with the Ethics Policy Committee, several lengthy meetings with each of the two law firms which were serving as outside legal counsel, a joint meeting with Society leaders, and countless informal meetings of shorter duration. In addition to participating in meeting discussions, committee members spent literally hundreds of hours studying proposed revisions and preparing written evaluations at various stages in the process. Detailed written legal opinions were obtained from both law firms. Finally, the documents were ready to distribute to all members of the Board of Trustees of the American Institute. It was a satisfying day, in retrospect, despite the remaining imperfections in the proposed code.

There had been many problems and issues to resolve along the way. The legal problems alone had been perplexing enough.[79] The Institute Bylaws had to be revised extensively. Disciplinary rules, procedures, and penalties had to be structured to comply with constitutional due

---

79. Those who are interested in the legal problems associated with professional ethics codes will find excellent summaries in Earl W. Kintner, Esq., "Legal Limitations and Possibilities for Self-Enforcement of Codes of Ethics," *The Ethical Basis of Economic Freedom,* op. cit., pp. 387-402; and George D. Webster, *The Law of Associations,* Rev. 2nd ed., 1974, Matthew Bender & Co., Inc., esp. Ch. No. IX, "Code of Ethics," pp. 143-52.

process requirements and other dictates of the law, as well as to meet common-sense notions of reasonableness, equity, and fairness. And there were many other legal and insurance problems which are well beyond the scope of this essay.

Perhaps the most difficult drafting problem was posed by the enormous diversity within the CPCU group. In this respect, the Institute is not alone. The ethics codes in law and accounting frequently have been criticized for their failure to address the unique ethics problems of CPAs and lawyers who are employed by corporations.[80] Even so, the Institute problem is probably more acute, because CPCUs include persons who are agents, brokers, underwriters, claims representatives, safety engineers, university teachers, insurance regulators, company executives, corporate risk managers, and many other insurance and insurance-related specialists. To accommodate such diversity, many specific rules had to be generalized, and this, in turn, made them more difficult to interpret.

A practical but important issue had to do with the familiar question of "grandfathering." Counsel had advised that the Institute could legally impose disciplinary sanctions (including suspension or revocation of the privilege to use the CPCU designation) on any CPCU who violated an ethics Rule, regardless of whether the violator had received his or her designation prior to the date of the Code adoption, since, from the legal point of view, the code was just a revision of the CPCU Charge. The Trustees did adopt the full range of disciplinary sanctions legally available (as described later), but they were persuaded by nonlegal considerations in resolving the "grandfather" issue. Accordingly, the ethics Rules were made binding and enforceable, as of the Code's effective date (June 18, 1976), on (1) all CPCU candidates, and (2) all CPCUs whose designations will be conferred after the effective date of the Code. For CPCUs whose designations were conferred *prior* to the Code's effective date, the so-called "grandfathers," the ethics Rules were made enforceable only on individual CPCUs who first file a voluntary written election to be bound by the mandates of the Rules.[81] As of this writing, thousands of CPCUs have filed such voluntary written elections to be bound. Thousands have not.

Mandatory continuing education proved to be another difficult issue.

---

80. For example, see Carl A. Pierce, "The Code of Professional Responsibility in the Corporate World: An Abdication of Professional Self-Regulation," *Journal of Law Reform,* Winter 1973, Vol. 6, pp. 350-74. Also see Stephen E. Loeb, "A Code of Ethics for CPAs in Industry: A Survey," *The Journal of Accountancy,* December 1971, pp. 52-60.
81. See the Preamble, Code of Professional Ethics of the American Institute for Property and Liability Underwriters, Inc., effective June 18, 1976.

The Ad Hoc and Ethics Policy Committees favored an ethics Rule which would have required all CPCUs to select and complete, within each three-year interval, their choice from among specified types and hours of approved continuing education activities. Failure to do so would have been grounds for disciplinary action, although the Rule would have stopped short of the CPAs' approach of requiring periodic certification or proof of compliance. After considerable discussion, the Rule was generalized to read: "A CPCU shall keep informed on those technical matters that are essential to the maintenance of the CPCU's professional competence in insurance, risk management, or related fields."[82] This Rule is considerably less demanding than the continuing education requirements in public accounting and medicine. The Rule is an important step forward, though, because it officially recognizes continuing education as an *ethical* obligation of all CPCUs.

Heading the list of controversial issues was the question of whether the ethics Rules should apply to matters of personal conduct and morality. There was total agreement on the need to deal with matters of professional and business conduct (including the conduct of CPCUs in noninsurance businesses). The issue was whether the Institute should become involved in seemingly "personal" matters like parking tickets, marital infidelity, the use of illegal drugs, or other similar activities which, according to opponents of Institute involvement, have little to do with a CPCU's professional competence and *professional* ethics. After much debate, the pertinent Rule became: "A CPCU will be subject to disciplinary action for the *violation of any law* or regulation, to the extent that such violation suggests the likelihood of *professional* misconduct in the future." (emphasis supplied)[83] The aspirational standards also admonish CPCUs to avoid *any* conduct or activity which would cause *unjust harm to others.*

Still another difficult question was whether or not CPCUs should be ethically obligated to report the misconduct of another CPCU. The ethics code in medicine obligates a physician to expose, without hesitation, the illegal or unethical conduct of another physician. The CPCU Code does not go quite that far.[84] It forbids a CPCU from initiating or supporting the CPCU candidacy of a person known to engage in practices which violate the Code. It obligates a CPCU to furnish information *when officially requested* to do so by the proper Institute ethics authority. And it obligates a CPCU to report promptly to the Institute the use of the CPCU designation by an unauthorized person. Otherwise, it does not *require* a CPCU voluntarily to report a violation, sign a formal

---

82. The Code, Rules of Professional Conduct, R2.1.
83. Ibid., R3.3.
84. See Rules R9.1, R9.2 and R9.3.

complaint, or testify in a disciplinary hearing. These latter matters are left to individual professional judgments.

A number of professions have ethics rules which effectively prohibit one member from criticizing another member of the profession. The Ad Hoc Committee felt strongly that such provisions are contrary to the public interest. Thus, the Code Rules prohibit "any act or omission of a dishonest, deceitful or fraudulent nature" (R3.1) and misrepresentations or concealments of "any limitations on the CPCU's ability to provide the quantity or quality of professional services required by the circumstances" (R6.3). The aspirational standards also caution CPCUs against conduct which would cause *unjust* harm to others, and they encourage CPCUs to establish dignified and honorable relationships with fellow insurance practitioners.

A Rule also obligates the CPCU to "competently and consistently discharge his or her occupational duties" (R4.1). Yet, the disciplinary actions for violating the ethical obligation of diligent performance had to be qualified in carefully-drafted Guidelines, so that the Institute would not become an intervenor or arbitrator in contractual or civil disputes with employers, principals, or clients (see G4.1).

Another problem centered on the desirability of obligating CPCUs to encourage other qualified individuals to pursue the CPCU designation. The Code of the American Society of CLU contains a similar provision for CLUs, in the belief that it is in the interest of the insuring public. The latter belief found some support among members of the Institute's Ad Hoc Committee. But the majority felt strongly that a narrow version of the notion would be entirely self-serving, and that the public interest would be better served by the concept which obligates CPCUs to assist in maintaining and raising professional standards in the insurance business (Canon 5). Hence, the binding Rule became: "A CPCU shall encourage and assist qualified individuals *who wish to pursue* CPCU *or other studies* which will enhance their professional competence" (R5.2, emphasis supplied).

Heated debate was provoked by a proposal to follow the lead of medicine and obligate CPCUs to share the benefits of their professional attainments with other insurance practitioners (e.g., by writing articles or by teaching education and training classes). Opponents felt that such a rule would obligate CPCUs to divulge trade secrets and knowledge which give them a competitive advantage. The compromise took the form of rules requiring CPCUs to *support efforts* to improve the public understanding of insurance and risk management.

Finally, two somewhat related issues concerned the relative importance of disciplinary sanctions and the difficulties in teaching ethics. Some organizations take the view that, as long as there are appropriate disciplinary rules, procedures, and penalties, the ethics standards should be brief and simple, thus leaving matters of interpretation largely up to the judgment of a disciplinary tribunal. The Ad Hoc Committee acknowledged the importance of disciplinary rules and penalties, but it categorically rejected the idea that the ethics standards should be brief and simple and interpretable mostly by a disciplinary tribunal. First and foremost, brief and simple standards would not meet the educational and other objectives which had been given the greatest weight. As to the less important objective of punishing violators, moreover, it seems grossly unfair to rely on ethics standards for which written interpretations are not available to those subject to the code. Thus, the Institute opted for a longer list of code standards, and it decided to make a concerted effort to publish a variety of materials to assist CPCUs and CPCU candidates in interpreting the code provisions. This is in keeping with the broad goal of *fostering* ethical conduct and practices.

A few opponents of the code suggested that "ethics cannot be taught." Actually, ethics is a branch of philosophy which has been successfully taught since the days of Socrates. Professional ethics is now being taught, with excellent overall results, in law schools, business schools, and industry training programs.[85] While it is probably true that the study of ethics will not, by itself, turn "all the bad people into good people," it can most certainly remove the intellectual barriers to ethical conduct, and it is likely to have desirable side effects on the conduct of all who are required to engage in the effort. There is likewise an element of truth in Oscar Wilde's notion that nothing worth knowing is capable of being taught. It must be learned. As Edward Gibbon observed: "Every man who rises above the common level has received two educations: the first from his teachers; the second, more personal and important, from himself." This truth will not be altered by the critics of ethics codes.

Among the problems and issues described above, some had to be resolved by compromise. None of the controversial notions were thrown out of the code draft entirely. Some were modified to make them acceptable as Rules, whereas the others were changed into broader, aspira-

---

85. For a few examples, see Frank E. Maloney, "Practicing Lawyers Teach Ethics at University of Florida," *The Florida Bar Journal*, January 1973, Vol. 47, No. 1, pp. 14-16; Robert H. Aronson, "New Dimensions in Legal Ethics," *Learning and the Law*, Fall 1975, pp. 50-54; Marvin W. Mindes, "Forcing an Identity Crisis On Law Students," *Learning and the Law*, Fall 1975, pp. 44-47; "Law Schools Casual Ethics Attitude Must End," *American Bar News*, July 1974; Ron Zemke, "Ethics Training: Can We Really Teach People Right from Wrong," *Training HRD*, May 1977, pp. 37-41; and Nathan A. Baily, "The Role of Business and Business Schools in Raising Ethical Standards in Business," *The National Public Accountant*, Vol. 14, No. 6, June 1969, pp. 4-6.

tional standards. The documents were now ready to submit to those who would make the final decisions.

Code Approval

On June 17, 1976, the Executive Committee of the Board of Trustees met to consider the Code draft and the implementing recommendations related thereto, including the proposed changes in the Institute's Bylaws. These materials had been distributed to all the Trustees one month earlier, and some changes had already been made in accordance with suggestions of individual Trustees. Additional changes were made by the Executive Committee, during a lengthy session of careful deliberations. It was both obvious and gratifying that the members of the Institute's Executive Committee did not take their responsibilities lightly.

The next day, the revised Code draft and recommendations were presented to the full Board of Trustees. Numerous questions were raised by the Trustees, who had obviously done their homework prior to the meeting. It was an hour which seemed like a month. Then came the moment which every CPCU in this and future generations can be proud of. The Trustees voted *unanimously* to adopt the recommendations and the new Code of Professional Ethics.

It was not and is not a perfect code. It is a comprehensive code of the type which was (and is) sorely needed. As John Stuart Mill said so many years ago, the virtue of having an ethics code is one of those truths which kept reappearing until it had "made such head as to withstand all subsequent attempts to suppress it." It now needs to be improved through experience and enlightened criticism.

General Nature of the Code

Since all CPCU candidates are required to study the Code in its entirety, the description here will be brief and general in nature. The Preamble should be read carefully, because it explains the nature and purpose of the various kinds of standards and published ethics materials.

The Code of Professional Ethics consists of the Preamble, nine Canons, and twenty-four Rules of Professional Conduct. The Canons are broad concepts of an aspirational nature, whereas the Rules are specific standards, of an enforceable nature, which prescribe the minimum levels of required professional conduct. The Guidelines for the use of the

CPCU designation and CPCU key have been incorporated by reference into a Rule (R8.1) and are thus enforceable.

The Rules are numbered and grouped schematically under a Canon with which they are closely associated; however, there are some very important interrelationships between and among the various kinds of standards. This will become readily apparent when candidates begin to work with the ethics case studies and attempt to apply the Code to given factual situations. In the usual case, the conduct in question will involve several Canons, Rules, and Guidelines, and it must be evaluated in the general context of the entire Code.

Canon 1 sets the general theme and purpose of the entire code, by admonishing CPCUs to "endeavor at all times to place the *public* interest above their own." How do CPCUs do that, i.e., how do they serve the public interest? They do it by strictly observing all the enforceable Rules, at a minimum, and by striving to meet the higher standards contained in the Canons and Guidelines.

The General Nature of Code-Related Materials

In addition to the Preamble, Canons and Rules of the code itself, there are forty published Guidelines for Professional Conduct, twenty published Advisory Opinions of the Board of Ethical Inquiry (each dealing with an ethics case study), and published Disciplinary Rules and Procedures. The Guidelines and Advisory Opinions are designed to assist CPCUs and CPCU candidates in interpreting the various code provisions, understanding their rationale and applying them to frequently-encountered situations which require ethical judgments. The Guidelines, Advisory Opinions, and Canons also may be used in interpreting the Rules and applying them in actual disciplinary cases brought before the Board of Ethical Inquiry or other duly authorized tribunal.

The Disciplinary Rules and Procedures are designed to meet the constitutional requirements concerning due process of law, protect the rights of the accused, and meet other common-sense standards of decency and fairness, while at the same time making it possible to impose reasonable penalties upon those who violate specific Rules in the code. With respect to CPCU candidates and applicants who violate a Rule, admission to any examination and the awarding of the CPCU designation may be withheld indefinitely, pending receipt of convincing proof of the violator's full and complete rehabilitation. With respect to CPCUs who are subject to the binding effect of the Rules, a Rule violation may lead to a *private admonition* requesting the violator to cease and desist, a *reprimand* or informal rebuke given limited publication, a *censure* or formal rebuke given wide publication, or the *suspension or revocation of the privilege to use the CPCU designation,* for a probationary period or indefinitely, with or without publication. Of course, the Board of Ethical Inquiry may refuse to hear a case (e.g., where no formal written complaint has been signed) or it may dismiss a case on its merits.

The New Ethics Organizational Structure

The Ad Hoc Committee on Professional Ethics, having discharged its responsibilities, was replaced by other committees in the Institute's new ethics organizational structure. The Registration Committee was also replaced. All Institute ethics activities are now handled entirely by the Ethics Policy Committee, the Board of Ethical Inquiry, and the Ethics Counsel of the American Institute.

Ethics Policy Committee The Ethics Policy Committee is now a standing committee of the Board of Trustees. The Ethics Policy Committee is responsible for reviewing matters of policy associated with all Institute ethics activities, making recommendations to the Executive Committee and the full Board of Trustees, and providing for liaison with the Society of CPCU on ethical policy considerations. The Ethics Policy Committee also is empowered to act on behalf of the Board in reviewing the penalties administered by the Board of Ethical Inquiry.

Board of Ethical Inquiry The Board of Ethical Inquiry (BEI) consists of eight members who are appointed by the President subject to the advice and consent of the Ethics Policy Committee. All members must be CPCUs, and together they must constitute, as nearly as is practical, a representative cross section of the occupational positions and other pertinent characteristics of all CPCUs. The Ethics Counsel must be a staff officer of the Institute, other than the President, and will serve as nonvoting chairman, Ex Officio. The other seven members of the Board of Ethical Inquiry cannot be full-time employees of the American Institute or the Society of CPCU.

Basically, the Board of Ethical Inquiry is responsible for implementing established and approved ethics policies. In many respects, the most important function of the BEI is to *encourage voluntary compliance with the code,* as well as continuing discussion, study, and criticism of it, by all CPCUs and CPCU candidates. The BEI issues informal and formal published Advisory Opinions to CPCUs and matriculated CPCU candidates who request assistance in interpreting or applying the code; it promulgates and publishes Guidelines to supplement the code; it approves the content of ethics materials to be used in the CPCU curriculum for study by candidates; it answers all correspondence pertaining to ethics; it summarizes and publishes rulings in cases brought before the disciplinary tribunals; and, it serves a liaison on ethics activities with other professional societies and organizations. The BEI also certifies that applicants have met the requirements for candidacy, and that candidates have met the ethics requirements for conferment of their CPCU designations. It is obligated to make *recommendations* concerning changes in the code, changes in the Disciplinary Rules and Procedures, changes in ethics policies and the budget and staff it requires to carry out its functions.

In its code enforcement capacities, the BEI receives complaints, instigates independent investigations of the facts, serves as a tribunal to hear and decide cases, and imposes such penalties as are warranted and available to the BEI. The BEI may carry out some of its functions through outside legal counsel, Institute staff, consultants, investigators or subcommittees, but all disciplinary actions and published materials, other than routine correspondence, must be approved by a majority of its voting members.

Except as otherwise noted above, no Institute staff member, officer, or Trustee has any authority to speak or act *on behalf of the American Institute* on ethics and specific ethics-related matters, nor does any officer, staff member, Trustee, or member of the Society of CPCU. These are vital safeguards to assure uniformity and equity in interpreting the code, protect the rights and interests of those subject to the code, reserve the disciplinary and interpretative functions for duly authorized bodies, and otherwise serve the interests of the general public.

AN EPILOGUE

One has the irrepressible urge, for the sake of emphasis, to repeat several points already made in earlier sections of this essay. First, the idea of a profession, as a distinctive occupational group, is best defined by identifying its collective set of desirable characteristics. Since individuals within the group may or may not meet the tests of profession status, such characteristics have their greatest value as definers of standards which each individual may seek to achieve. The most essential qualities of professionalism are high standards of professional *competence* and professional *ethics*. Accordingly, the true professional is an individual who (1) has a high level of professional competence and (2) adheres to high ethical standards in the maintenance and application of that competence.

Although there are knowledge and skill ingredients in virtually every occupation, the required blend of the two will vary among occupations. In insurance, as with other occupations, professional "competence" needs to be more sharply defined. The same can be said of professional "ethics," which has been defined largely by the written codes of professional ethics which have been adopted for hundreds of occupations and professional organizations. It helps a great deal to understand that competence, professionalism, and ethics are dialectical terms. To define them at all, one must take sides. One must indulge in the ancient art of rhetoric, argument in pursuit of truth.

All codes of professional ethics need to be improved. In particular, they need to lay greater stress on the larger public interest, the common good. They also need to be revised, periodically, to keep pace with the critical issues of a rapidly changing and increasingly complex society.

The new Code of Professional Ethics of the American Institute marks the beginning of a new era of insurance professionalism. All current CPCUs and CPCU candidates can be justifiably proud to be part of this monumental development in insurance history. Even so, every true insurance professional will not yet be satisfied. Each will have an insatiable appetite to reach higher plateaus of professionalism, if only because people must care for others if they are ultimately to care for themselves.

Selected Bibliography

AICPA Professional Standards, Vol. 2, 1976. Published for the American Institute of Certified Public Accountants by Commerce Clearing House, Inc.

Anderson, Ronald T. "The Professional Urge." *CPCU Annals,* Vol. 29, No. 6, June 1976, pp. 116-22.

Arnold, Ralph. "Living With Unfair Claims Practices Acts." *Best's Review,* Property/Liability Edition, June 1975.

Aronson, Robert H. "New Dimensions in Legal Ethics." *Learning and the Law,* Fall 1975, pp. 50-54.

Baily, Nathan A. "The Role of Business and Business Schools in Raising Ethical Standards in Business." *The National Public Accountant,* Vol. 14, No. 6, June 1969, pp. 4-6.

Beamer, Elmer G. "Continuing Education—A Professional Requirement." *The Journal of Accountancy,* January 1972, pp. 33-39.

Belth, Joseph M. "Observations on the Enforcement Machinery of the C.L.U. Code of Ethics." *The Journal of Risk and Insurance,* March 1974, pp. 171-78.

Brandon, Lawrence G. "Value Orientations of Insurance Industry Chief Executives: A Study of the Identification and Role of Personal Values in Decision Making." *CPCU Annals,* Vol. 29, No. 3, September 1976, pp. 205-12.

Brandow, William E. "Insurance as a Profession." *CPCU Annals,* Vol. 17, No. 4, Winter 1964, pp. 374-75.

C.F.A. Readings in Financial Analysis, 1st ed. Homewood, IL: Richard D. Irwin, 1966.

Chittick, Ralph J. "Responsibilities of Professionalism." *The Journal of the American Society of CLU,* Winter 1964, pp. 29-40.

Cleaver, Denis A. "Consumerism to Destruction? A Company Man's View." *CPCU Annals,* Vol. 27, No. 4, December 1974, pp. 322-23.

Code of Professional Responsibility. American Bar Association, 1970, published by the Pennsylvania Bar Association, 1974.

Cogan, Morris L. "The Problem of Defining a Profession." *The Annals of the American Academy of Political and Social Science,* January 1955, pp. 105-11.

Cogan, Morris L. "Toward a Definition of Profession." *Harvard Educational Review,* Vol. XXIII, No. 1, Winter 1953, pp. 33-50.

Daenzer, Bernard John. "Ethics and Insurance," *Ethics for Modern Business Practice.* J. Whitney Bunting, ed. Englewood Cliffs, NJ: Prentice-Hall, 1953.

Decaminada, Joseph, P. "Code of Ethics of The Society of CPCU." *CPCU Annals,* Vol. 29, No. 3, September 1976, pp. 169-71.

Douglas, Patricia P. "Professionalism: Its Presence and Absence in the Insurance Industry." *The Journal of Risk and Insurance,* Vol. XXXVIII, No. 2, June 1971, pp. 218-24.

Dowell, C. Dwayne, and Anderson, Wilton T. "CPA Requirements of the States." *Collegiate News and Views,* Vol. XXXI, No. 1, Fall 1977.

"Ethical Principles in the Conduct of Research with Human Participants." Washington, D.C.: American Psychological Assn., 1973.

Ethical Standards of Psychologists. American Psychological Assn., 1953.

"First Interim Report on Mandatory Continuing Legal Education." Committee on Continuing Legal Education, State Bar of Michigan. *Michigan State Bar Journal,* October 1975, pp. 762-67.

Fish, Stan. "Keep the Renaissance Moving." *CPCU Annals,* Vol. 27, No. 3, September 1974, pp. 232-34.

Friedman, Milton. *Capitalism and Freedom,* 5th impression. Chicago & London: The University of Chicago Press, 1965, esp. Ch. IX, "Occupational Licensure."

Gallup, George. "The Gallup Opinion Index, Political, Social and Economic Trends." Report No. 134, September 1976, pp. 17-29.

Garrett, T.; Baumhart, Raymond; Purcell, Theodore; and Poets, Perry. *Cases in Business Ethics.* New York: Appleton-Century-Crofts, 1968.

Granger, George L. "State Licensing Requirements for Insurance Agents and Brokers." *CPCU Annals,* Vol. 27, No. 2, June 1974, pp. 128-36.

Hayes, Douglas A. "Potential for Profession Status." *Financial Analysts Journal,* November-December 1967, pp. 29-31.

Hazlett, Henry. "The Ethics of Capitalism." *The Foundations of Morality.* D. Van Nostrand Co., Inc., 1964, reprinted by the Education Division of the National Association of Manufacturers, 1965.

Higgins, Thomas G., and Olson, Wallace, E. "Restating the Ethics Code: A Decision for the Times." *The Journal of Accountancy,* March 1972, pp. 33-39.

Hill, Ivan, ed. *The Ethical Basis of Economic Freedom,* Plus special commentaries on Codes of Ethics and how they work. Chapel Hill, NC: American Viewpoint, 1976.

Horn, Ronald C., ed. & primary author. *Code of Professional Ethics of the American Institute,* effective June 18, 1976. Malvern, PA: American Institute for Property and Liability Underwriters, 1978.

Horn, Ronald C. "The Professions, Professionalism and the Professional." An address delivered at the local CLU diploma presentation exercises in Lansing, MI; Spokane, WA; Fresno, Bakersfield, Palo Alto, and San Jose, CA; and Cherry Hill, NJ.

Horn, Ronald C. "Higher than Higher Education: Some Unconventional Observations on What the Future Will Require of Insurance Professionals." A paper delivered at the 81st annual convention of the Independent Insurance Agents of Kentucky, November 15, 1977, Louisville, KY.

Horn, Ronald C. "Current Developments in the Property-Liability Insurance Industry: A Summary of Noteworthy Events and Possible Trends." Malvern, PA: Insurance Institute of America, 1970.

Horn, Ronald C. "The Artificial Hierarchy of Risk Management Theory and Practice." A paper presented to the 1972 annual meeting and seminars of the American Society of Insurance Management, Montreal, Canada.

Horn, Ronald C. "On Keeping Pace: The Continuing Education Challenge for Professional Risk Managers." A paper presented to the 1974 annual meeting and seminars of the American Society of Insurance Management, Toronto, Canada.

Horn, Ronald C. "How to Tell a Pure Estate Planner from a Lay Estate Planner: The Secret of Socrates Revisited." An address delivered at various seminars of Life Underwriter Associations and Estate Planning Councils in Kentucky and South Carolina.

Horn, Ronald C. "Claims Consciousness: A Dilemma in Perspective." A paper presented to the 1968 annual seminar of the South Carolina Claims Association.

Huebner, S.S. "The Professional Concept in Life Underwriting." Bryn Mawr, PA: The American College, edited in 1975.

Kelley, Augustus. *Moral Views of Commerce, Society and Politics.* New York: Orville Dewey, 1969.

Kemper, James S., Jr. "Business Accountability for Social Action." *CPCU Annals,* Vol. 27, No. 3, September 1974, pp. 235-36.

Ketchum, Marshall D. "Is Financial Analysis a Profession?" *Financial Analysts Journal,* November-December 1967, pp. 33-37.

Lawrence, Floyd G. "Whose Ethics Guide Business?" *Industry Week,* 27 October 1975.

"Law Schools' Casual Ethics Attitude Must End." *American Bar News,* July 1974.

Leveratt, E.J., Jr., and Trieschmann, James S. "Fees vs. Commissions: Are They Legal?" *CPCU Annals,* Vol. 27, No. 4, December 1974, pp. 266-70.

"Life Insurance Consumers." *LIAMA Research Report 1973-10,* file No. 940. A Review of the Literature by the Life Insurance Agency Management Association with The Institute of Life Insurance.

Loeb, Stephen E. "Enforcement of the Code of Ethics: A Survey." *The Accounting Review,* Vol. XLVII, No. 1, January 1972, pp. 1-10.

Loeb, Stephen E. "A Code of Ethics for CPAs in Industry: A Survey." *The Journal of Accountancy,* December 1971, pp. 52-60.

Long, John D. "Social Responsibility of Insurance Companies: A Point of View." *CPCU Annals,* Vol. 27, No. 3, September 1974, pp. 237-46.

Long, John D. "Insurance and the New Morality." *CPCU Annals,* December 1970, pp. 303-21.

McCullough, Roy C. "Professional Liability." *Issues in Insurance,* Vol. II. John D. Long, ed. Malvern, PA: American Institute for Property and Liability Underwriters, 1978.

MacIver, R.M. "The Social Significance of Professional Ethics." *The Annals of the American Academy of Political and Social Science,* January 1955, pp. 118-24.

Malecki, Donald; Donaldson, James; and Horn, Ronald C. *Commercial Liability Risk Management and Insurance.* Malvern, PA: American Institute for Property and Liability Underwriters, 1978.

Maloney, Frank E. "Practicing Lawyers Teach Ethics at University of Florida." *The Florida Bar Journal,* Vol. 47, No. 1, January 1974, pp. 14-16.

May, Gordon S. "Continuing Professional Education—Required or Voluntary." *The Journal of Accountancy,* August 1975, pp. 110-13.

Mindes, Marvin W. "Forcing an Identity Crisis on Law Students." *Learning and the Law,* Fall 1975, pp. 44-47.

"Monitoring Attitudes of the Public." American Council of Life Insurance, 1976.

Morrison, Robert M. "The Anomalous Position of the Insurance Agent—An Invitation to Schizophrenia." *Villanova Law Review,* Spring 1967, pp. 535-44.

Murphy, Thomas A. "A Businessman's Concern for Freedom." St Louis: Beta Gamma Sigma, 1974.

O'Neill, Eileen Creamer. "Creating and Promoting a Code of Ethics." *Association Management,* November 1972, pp. 44-50.

Overman, Edwin S. *The Professional Concept And Business Ethics.* Malvern, PA: American Institute for Property and Liability Underwriters.

Overman, Edwin S. "What Does It Really Require to be Professional?" CPCU Conferment Address, 1977.

Palmer, Russell E. "It's Time to Stop Talking." *The Journal of Accountancy,* October 1975, pp. 60-65.

Parker, Douglas H. "Periodic Recertification of Lawyers—A Comparative Study of Programs for Maintaining Professional Competence." *Michigan State Bar Journal,* October 1975, pp. 768-95; reprinted from the *Utah Law Review,* No. 3, Fall 1974.

Paton, W.A. "Earmarks of a Profession—And the APB." *The Journal of Accountancy,* January 1971, pp. 37-45.

Peet, William. "Insurance—Present or Potential Profession." *CPCU Annals,* Vol. 13, No. 2, Fall 1960, pp. 165-72.

Peet, William. "A Profession for CPCUs." *CPCU Annals,* Vol. 16, No. 1, Spring 1963, pp. 82-87.

Pierce, Carl A. "The Code of Professional Responsibility in the Corporate World—An Abdication of Professional Self-Regulation." *Journal of Law Reform,* Vol. 16, Winter 1973, pp. 350-74.

"Principles of Medical Ethics." Chicago: The American Medical Association, 1974 printing.

Pritchard, William G. "Social Responsibility in the Insurance Marketplace." *CPCU Annals,* Vol. 27, No. 1, March 1974, pp. 46-48.

"Report of the State Bar Grievance Board." *Michigan State Bar Journal,* September 1975, pp. 720-22.

Royster, Vermont. "The Common Behavior." *Wall Street Journal,* Editorial, 17 September 1975.

Russell, G. Hugh, and Black, Kenneth, Jr. "Professional Selling and Non-Verbal Communications." *The Journal of the American Society of C.L.U.,* Winter 1964, pp. 21-28.

Sager, William H. "Rules of Professional Conduct—Self-Discipline or Self-Complacency." *The National Public Accountant,* March 1970, pp. 4-11.

Schafer, John S. "American Insurance: The Consumer's View." *CPCU Annals,* Vol. 27, No. 2, June 1974, pp. 143-47.

Shay, Philip W. *Ethics and Professional Conduct in Management Consulting.* New York: Association of Consulting Management Engineers, 1965.

Sheppard, C. Stewart. "The Professionalization of the Financial Analyst." *Financial Analysts Journal,* November-December 1967, pp. 39-41.

Smith, Robert Houston. "New Directions for Ethical Codes." *Association and Society Manager,* December/January 1973-74, pp. 124-28.

Smith, Willis A. "The Revised AICPA Rules of Conduct—To Serve the Public Interest." *The CPA Journal,* November 1973, pp. 963-68.

Snider, H. Wayne. "Problems of Professionalism." *The Journal of Insurance,* Vol. XXX, No. 4, December 1963, pp. 563-72.

Sprague, W.D. "The Case for Universal Professional Development." *The CPA Journal,* September 1973, pp. 747-53.

"State Ethics Codes Applied to Campuses." *The Chronicle of Higher Education,* Vol. XII, No. 13, 24 May 1976.

Stern, Duke N., and Klock, David R. "Public Policy and the Professionalization of Life Underwriters." *American Business Law Journal,* Vol. 13, 1975, pp. 225-38.

Strother, George. "The Moral Codes of Executives—A Watergate-Inspired Look at Barnard's Theory of Executive Responsibility." *Academy of Management Review,* Vol. 1, No. 2, April 1976.

"Study Finds Lack of Clergy Ethics Code: Tells Contemporary Concern." *National Catholic Reporter,* 16 January 1976, p. 15.

Tannenbaum v. Provident Mutual Life Ins. Co., 53 App. Div. 2d 86, 386 N.Y.S. 2d 409 (1976), aff'd mem, No. 218, 5 May 1977. Special duty of care for a CLU.

"The Study of American Opinion." *U.S. News & World Report,* 2nd annual survey of public attitudes.

"The Principles of Medical Ethics with Annotations Especially Applicable to Psychiatry." *American Journal of Psychiatry,* Vol. 130, No. 9, September 1973, pp. 1058-62.

Towe, Joseph W., et al. *Ethics and Standards in American Business.* Boston: Houghton Mifflin, 1964.

U.S. Department of Commerce. "Occupations of Persons with High Earnings." 1970 Census of Population, Social, and Economic Statistics Administration.

U.S. Department of Labor. *Dictionary of Occupational Titles,* 4th ed. 1977, Employment and Training Administration.

Very, Donald L. "The Pennsylvania Unfair Insurance Practices Act: The Sleeping Giant." *CPCU Annals,* Vol. 28, No. 2, June 1975, pp. 109-16.

Wall Street Journal, report on ethics survey of business executives, 10 June 1975.

Watson, Robert I. *Psychology as a Profession.* New York: Doubleday, 1954.

Weaver, Richard. *The Ethics of Rhetoric.* 1st Gateway ed. Chicago: Henry Regnery Co., 1967.

Webster, George D. *The Law of Associations,* rev. 2nd ed., Matthew Bender & Co., 1974, esp. Ch. No. IX, "Code of Ethics," pp. 143-52.

Whitehead, Alfred North. *Adventures of Ideas.* New York: Macmillan, 1933, pp. 72-73.

Zemke, Ron. "Ethics Training: Can We Really Teach People Right from Wrong." *Training HRD,* May 1977, pp. 37-41.

Index